Tempus ORAL HISTORY *Series*

Fairford and Lechlade
voices

The author as a child, with her brother, Leslie, mother (on right) and Granny Lewis.

Tempus ORAL HISTORY *Series*

Fairford and Lechlade
voices

Compiled by
June Lewis-Jones

TEMPUS

First published 2001
Copyright © June Lewis-Jones, 2001

Tempus Publishing Limited
The Mill, Brimscombe Port,
Stroud, Gloucestershire, GL5 2QG

ISBN 0 7524 2272 3

Typesetting and origination by
Tempus Publishing Limited
Printed in Great Britain by
Midway Colour Print, Wiltshire

For Katherine and Andrew

Fairford Market Place, 1804 (taken from old engraving).

Contents

Acknowledgements

My initial thanks must go to all the people who have contributed their memories, stories and thoughts that make up this book and produced valued personal photographs – I am extremely grateful to each and every one for their interest and candour.

In addition to all those who are listed as contributors, I must add special thanks to Helen Thomas, Dr Harold Bloxsome's daughter, for so generously allowing me to use extracts from her father's autobiographical notes; to Jose Newman, for agreeing to my using my interview of her mother, Mrs Winifred May; to Susan Vicary, for tracing such interesting information on the Bazley family; and to John Bennett, for raiding the family albums for photographs.

To David and Jane Pitts, my special thanks for guiding my tentative steps into the world of computer technology; to LaVelle, for her encouragement to explore further into its mysteries; and, a huge thank-you to John Pursch, who so calmly unscrambles my tangles with the said technology.

Thank you, too, to my husband, Ralph, for his unfailing encouragement and support and finally, but by no means least, to my publishers, for their patience in getting the book to publication.

Lechlade Halfpenny Pike Bridge, c. 1790 (taken from old engraving).

Introduction

What a pleasure it has been to gather together this collection of reminiscences from local people, particularly because they are local to me and have or still people my own life. The greatest difficulty has been to select the contributors, and this was done without prejudice or personal interest, simply on the grounds of trying to get as wide a spectrum as possible within such a small area as the neighbouring old market towns of Fairford and Lechlade – barely four miles apart in the south-eastern corner of the Cotswolds.

In close proximity they may be, but the two places have distinctly different characteristics which have evolved from comparable origins. Both are very small market towns, each little larger than a big village, but with ancient charters for trading thus giving them a higher parish status, and it is this, above all else, that has imbued each with its unique community spirit. Archaeological evidence reveals both were sizeable settlements in Saxon times and even earlier, and documentary records span over a millennium, but it is the voices of the people who live and work here that speak to us of the many-faceted aspects of life yesterday and today in these two communities.

I have endeavoured to capture the character of each of the contributors as this gives the colour and cadence to their stories, just as if they were talking in print. It is their individuality – whether it be by age or experience – that makes this, in a way, a privileged insight into their lives. They provide huge chunks of social history that never make it into the analytical history books; but are of more value to a total understanding of an era or situation and our own place in the whole order of things, than a catalogue of dates and retrospective summing-up of causes, reasons and results. By the same token, I have cast my net to take in a story of life as it was, and is, in the 'big house' of two neighbouring villages, both of which have close affinity with the two towns.

Likewise, I have not confined my recording of life here to 'the way we were' – we are making history every single day, and that is why I felt it more important to include a glimpse of the flooding of last winter than a repeat of a Civil War skirmish, and the current thoughts of a young farmer and vet of a rural community caught up in the national crisis of foot-and-mouth disease, rather than a look back at the agricultural riots of yesteryear.

Here, then, is not a history of Fairford and Lechlade in the accepted sense, but a chat with some of the people who have, and still, contribute to making them not just beautiful and interesting old market towns – but home. So, for those to whom they still are, and for those who wish to be reminded of their roots, and for those who may just chance upon us at some time – just listen through the following pages to the voices of Fairford and Lechlade.

June Lewis-Jones
September 2001

CHAPTER 1
Childhood

Winifred May, aged sixteen.

A Century of Change

I suppose it is strange to think I was born during Queen Victoria's reign and that I have seen six monarchs on the throne, well, that includes Edward VIII, but he wasn't ever crowned as King. Some people say to me that they don't want to live to be 100, but life is sweet at any age as long as you keep well. I won a lot of prizes for needlework when I was at school. One day the vicar came and asked for me. I was worried that I had done something wrong – you were frightened of the vicar in those days, especially as he had so much say in the school. 'Winifred Churchman,' he said, 'if you can sew as well as that you can darn my surplice.' He must have been pleased with it because he gave me a shilling. A shilling was a lot in those days. We had inspectors come to the school and you had to work really hard to get through the exams. I earned 7s 6d one year for passing all mine, and that paid the fare for three of us, my mother, sister and myself, to go to Norfolk to relations for a little holiday. On Friday nights my mum and I helped make the faggots for Mrs Spencer's shop in Milton Street. We minced up the offal and herbs and mixed them in a big galvanized bath then had to wrap each small handful in a square of caul, a kind of lacy membrane from the pig. Those faggots smelled lovely when they were cooking and the women would come with their basins or jugs and sit in the little passageway – they used to call it Pug's Parlour – for their Friday night faggots and peas.

My father was a coach smith for Constables, that later became Busby's Garage, he made the springs and wheels for the old horse-drawn wagons and coaches. I remember my dad in the first car, it had wooden wheels and no roof. He was very good at music, my dad, he started the Fairford Silver Band and must have taught hundreds of young men to play over the years. Colonel Palmer at the Park bought all the first instruments and uniforms – the Band was a sight and sound to behold and played at all the big events in the town.

Yes, what a lot of changes there has been in my lifetime. When I was young we never dreamt that there would be cars like there are now, and aeroplanes, let alone men walking on the moon!

Winifred May

Schooldays

Our house in Lechlade was just opposite the church and I am told the bell-ringing lulled me to sleep. Apparently I would swing on the church gate and announce to all passers-by

The Hicks family of Lechlade.

The Warner family of Lechlade.

that I would be going to school 'when the cuckoo comes'. Sure enough, aged four and a half, I made the daily walk through the churchyard to the elementary school as it was called in those days. My first teacher was Miss Watkins, a little Welsh lady who told Mother that she despaired of my ever learning to blow my nose properly. She was less than impressed with my knitting skills, too. They did improve later when my younger sister, Janis, was born for whom I learnt to knit jumpers and cardigans.

From the infant classes I moved to the 'big school' – this was simply two adjacent classrooms. The top class was taken by the headmaster, Mr H.P. Harrison, a tall, well-built man whose voice could strike terror in our hearts. He had been wounded during service in the Great War and his uncertain temper and idiosyncrasies were attributed to

his experiences, but he was an extremely good teacher. I can't help feeling that the instruction we received compared very favourably with that of today. At the age of ten I was familiar with more than one Shakespearian play.

I also remember a lecture from the author, S.P.B. Mais, on the subject of the source of the River Thames – which, of course, flowed along the bottom of our playing field, and in bad winters flooded most of our back playground. The standard of our education was such that the eleven-plus examination held no particular terror for me and I completed my education at Cirencester Grammar School.

We looked forward to Lechlade Fair, the beautiful steam engine which supplied the power was parked by our house – it was magical, all lit up. It was so exciting to see the galloping horses, with their shining brass poles speeding round and round, and the swingboats and coconut shies. To finish the day we had the treat of a sixpenny packet of fish and chips from Mr Scarrott's shop on the corner of Thames Street.

I spent many a happy holiday time at my grandparents' Hall Court Farm. Grandma Warner, my mother's mother, was a Deacon – the Deacon family also had a dairy in Lechlade. I loved to watch Granny skimming the cream off the milk in huge shallow pans in the dairy, which was always terribly cold, and making butter in a big old churn. They sold skimmed milk for something like a ha'penny a pint. I loved helping to toss the hay in Leatherem – that was the field opposite the farm. That has been lost since the fifties when the new stretch of the Fairford road was made to cut off the narrow bend. Grandpa Warner went in for trotting horses and once had quite a famous one called Bonny Freda. His daughter, my Aunt

Winnie, who later became Mrs Eddolls, was very good with the horses, too. Most local people will have heard of Uncle Tom Warner, if only from the controversy which ran through the papers for so long on the housing development on what has become known as Tom Warner's field. It is good to see the old house, which had got into terrible disrepair over the last few years, has been restored. I still have the old family bible where all the names and dates were entered, and I see Tom Warner was born in 1896 and died on his birthday in 1984.

Beryl Law

Tales My Husband Told Me

Les was one of twelve surviving children, three others had died in infancy, and life in the Miller household in St John's Street was anything but dull. Looking back over

Tom Warner at the back of the cottage at Hall Court.

Lechlade School: Physical Training forties-style.

the years, Les recalled the kindly interest taken in the youngsters by the 'better off' ladies who gave a great deal of their time to help them in so many ways. Mrs Harrison, the headmaster's wife, took Bible classes and gave the boys their first experience of a County standard cricket match – a trip to Gloucester in the thirties was a wonderful outing. Then there was Miss Bluett, who suffered the heavy-handed and overzealous youth at play with her croquet set in her indefatigable attempt to introduce them to the more genteel pastimes, along with maypole-dancing on the lawn. The prowess of the pianist who accompanied the monthly 'pictures in the Hall' was held in high esteem – her appropriate trills and twiddles for the dramatic bits in the right places greatly enhanced the production of the latest cine-film released to the Lechlade village hall. What with the atmospheric music and the intermittent 'pinging' when the film broke, and the dulling effect of the droning whirr when it did run for any length of time – Friday night at the local 'flicks' was not to be missed at any price.

'Boss' Harrison, the headteacher, took a far less rosy-spectacled view of his charges – boys were just young men in the making to him. He always referred to young 'Froggie' Moss as the Admiral of Downington on account of the poor lad diving off the springboard at the bathing hut on the Gloucestershire side where the Thames had silted up on the bend. Emerging from the mud like a frog from hibernation, Froggie stuck as a name locally ever after.

Les went on the railway from school and became the youngest signalman in the country, but desperately wanted to join the Army and serve in the war like his brothers. His was a 'reserved occupation' so he couldn't be released, so he tried all manner of things to get the sack – even derailing an engine once, it didn't work. Not even a charge.

He certainly was more than a little puzzled by the oddity of the law – especially as his poor hard-working Mum was taken to the Magistrates' Court at Fairford for throwing a bowl of clean water in sheer exasperation over her neighbour during an ongoing dispute. She was fined 5s – a fortune in those days. The Magistrate told her that had she thrown slops from the chamber pot, instead of a bowl of clean water, she would have left with a caution instead!

Brenda Miller

Author's note

Extract from Magistrate's Court proceedings 1929: Fined half a crown and bound over to keep the peace at Fairford – Charlotte Westbury for drenching with dirty chamber water Ellen Maud Cowley at East End cottages.

Messrs Peyman – three generations. From left to right: Robert, Ian, Anthony, Clem, Michael, Stephen.

Twin Talk

We never used the fact that we are identical twins for any purpose or pranks. To be truthful, we were embarrassed about it when we were small, not here in Fairford because everyone knew us, but when we were away on holiday people would point us out: 'Oh, look, twins – how ever could you tell which is which'. We then got to walking on opposite sides of the road – Mike and Mum one side, Anthony and Dad the other. Of course, we have had many occasions of being mistaken for each other.

The Peymans have always been a family of cricketers. Once, when we were playing at South Hill, umpire Gough Cotterell was adamant that Mike returned to bat after he had been declared out. Anthony had to come out on to the field to show him that there really were two of us.

Mike has twin boys – Robert and Stephen, and he is glad that they are not alike, but like us, they are very close, but they are also close to Nicola their sister. But then, we are all a close-knit family. It is extraordinary that since we finished with the shop, which we had from 1953 to 1997, Mike now works at East Glos Engineering with Neil Kinch and Paul Warriner – and they are both one of a twin!

Anthony and Michael Peyman

Going Up To Farmor's

My twin brother and I left St Lawrence's Primary School at the end of the summer

Lechlade School, mid-sixties: staff and governors in front of the St Lawrence banner made by Dilys Hatton, when a teenager. Among her notable commissions as a professional embroiderer, was to make the stole for the Pope on his visit to England.

Farmor's Old School, c. 1930.

term in 1961, but he had passed the eleven-plus and was off to Cirencester Grammar School. One of the oldest of 80 children at Lechlade school, come September I would be bussed to Fairford and be one of the youngest of 250. The great day arrived and I dressed in my navy pleated skirt, royal blue jumper, white shirt and school tie – everyone wore a tie at that time – and navy blazer with the school badge stitched on to the pocket. I waited in Hambidge Lane for the school bus, which was known as Diesel Dick; it had seats like service buses today. Bert Titchener, the driver, was in a separate little cab. The boys made a rush for the back seats and we set off soon after 8 a.m.

I hadn't ever seen Farmor's School before, we didn't have the introductory days like the children have now. I remember the small yard at the back of the old stone building, which looked more like a big house in the High Street, children were pushing, shoving, laughing, shouting and trying to

play tag. A group of older girls had wedged themselves under the wooden stairs, no doubt discussing the older boys. Mr Bradley, the headmaster, came out as a hand-bell was rung and suddenly everything was quiet and still. All the new names were read out in classes and told where to go. The heavy wooden partition between the top rooms was pushed back so that everyone could get in for assembly. I had played my recorder every day at Lechlade and I took it with me that first morning, but I stuck it up my jumper in case I got laughed at. We were squashed in there tighter than in the playground, there was no room for a piano so everyone plunged into the hymn in a different key, then there was a prayer and some notices read out.

We spent more time in the following school days walking about than in class. Lessons were scattered around the place because the old school was really bursting at the seams with us all. We had to walk down

Farmor's School, built in Fairford Park in 1961.

Loders Field, late fifties: Chris Mattingley, Pat Hinton and Sarah Maundrell.

the Croft and into a narrow walled alley to get to the terrapin buildings by the infant school for domestic science, needlework, music and art. The boys did their woodwork there, too. The Palmer Hall was where we did our PE, but games were played at the other end of Fairford on the Coln House School playing field. At midday it was another walk for everyone to the Croft Chapel for dinner, which was served on the old altar.

After a month or so trailing around in all kinds of weather to get to our lessons, we were told that the new school in the Park was ready for us to move in. The teachers and pupils were still the same, but the new surroundings couldn't have been more different – there was suddenly so much space everywhere, inside and out. The hall took all of us, as well as a stage and a grand piano and there was still room for a small orchestra in front; it became the dining room at midday

Margaret Mattingley and Veronica Hemmings, teenage secretaries in Moore, Allen and Innocent's office during the mid-sixties.

Fairford Youth Fellowship – late forties. From left to right, the cast of A Quiet Weekend: *-?-, Mary Evans, Gill Edmonds, Robin Peat, Peggy Bridges, Dennis Bridges, Heather Powell, Peter Acock, Marjorie Heath, -?-, -?-, -?-, -?-, Joyce Morse.*

and the school dinners no longer came in big containers from Cirencester, they were cooked in the kitchen behind the hatch. The games field was huge and the gym well equipped. The proper science room had Bunsen burners and work benches round the walls. The domestic science room was all fitted out with brand new cookers and there was a little flat with sitting room, a bathroom and small kitchen, which we learnt to clean properly under the guidance of Mrs Williams. In our fourth year two or three of us would plan and cook a meal and invite a member of staff to dinner in the flat. The art room had a potter's wheel and a kiln, the library was lined with books and there were little cubicles for private study. Later, in one of the upstairs rooms, we had big new desks housing sturdy Imperial typewriters.

There was an ornamental pond where some pupils got a ducking if they passed by without being on their guard. We all had a form room with a desk or locker for our books and belongings. I felt privileged to be part of all this. It was a world away from the old school and all the walking up and down. I was sorry when schooldays ended for me in 1966 and I wept bitterly the day I left.

Margaret Mattingley

CHAPTER 2
Home

Rosemary Verey (kneeling centre) with son Charles at his christening tea party in the garden of Arden Cottage. From left to right, others: Emily Gibbs, Pat Sandilands (standing behind Rosemary), May Verey, Mrs Gibbs, Granny Verey.

A Model Cottage Garden

My husband, David, a captain in the Royal Fusiliers, was serving in the war and in 1942 I rented Arden Cottage in Fairford from Dr King Turner, senior. My rent at £1 a week was high for those days – especially as the cottage had been in such disrepair that we had to completely redec-orate it and put in a bathroom at our own expense. The iron railing fence separating the cottage from the main road was removed as part of the scrap iron war effort. The cottage was small – a sitting room and kitchen, and a tiny bedroom downstairs; two rooms upstairs plus our new bathroom.

The tall double doors on the right led

into the property where a large old *Lippia citriodora* (lemon scented verbena) grew. I had this moved, regretfully, so I could park our old Austin Ten, and then a pony trap. It was a model cottage garden; the kind you read about in Mrs Gaskell's novels, with a lawn, an old apple tree, beds for vegetables and, finally, an established asparagus bed, and then an area wired off for the chickens. Dr King Turner expected me to provide him with asparagus! Why should I – we enjoyed it and I paid a high rent for the cottage. Then, he had the audacity to accuse me of letting my sons – the eldest was two years old, the other just two months and still in a pram – steal the eggs from his geese in the next door field! I was furious and only twenty-three years old. I told him to get lost – this was in 1942 when we were <u>all</u> honest. We had a few ducks which laid big blue eggs, so I gave him some of those. His son Charlie and his wife were always very good friends of mine.

Other good, supportive friends were the Revd Francis Gibbs and his wife, Denise, who lived in the vicarage in London Street. In those days we could get to London very easily by train. I left my bicycle at Fairford Station and caught the train to Oxford, then on to London.

Memories of that home in Fairford will always stay with me – the gaslight, we had no electricity at that time. How much more personal the telephone system was, too. If I wanted a number and it was engaged the local operator just said, 'I am sorry, you may have to wait, but I will get you connected soon'.

Think back, it was only sixty years ago. How much has changed in our lifetime.

Rosemary Verey

Life At The Manor

When we came to view Kempsford Manor I stood at one of the bedroom windows and looked across the garden at the pond and I could see my whole life span played out before me. Charles had retired from the Diplomatic Service and he made a list of thirty-three reasons for not buying it: the roof, the plumbing – a really depressing catalogue of faults. I made a list of three: I love it; we must have it; I know we are going to live there – it's ordained! We moved here in 1977.

The Manor had already been separated: the lodge, stable cottage, and the west wing had been sold. The main house, purported to be eighteenth-century, remains something of an enigma – it was obvious that it had a complete makeover at that time, when we started work on renovating and decorating it appeared that at one time the first floor did not exist. We were going to make a doorway to lead from one room to another but came across roof joists at an angle. Also, whereas one reception room is typical of eighteenth-century design, the other two are completely different. The ancient deeds are in the Library of the Marquis of Bath – he owned most of the village as well as the estate at one time.

The original Manor House was on the site of the twelfth-century castle, nearer the church. The castle was the home of the Plantagenets, the centre of so much of the romance and history of the House of Lancaster – and, of course, Chaucer penning some of his poems there. When the castle fell into disrepair, the stone was taken by barge down the Thames to build Buscot Park. Manor Farmhouse replaced the old Manor House – and this house was built as the new one. We have the coat of

Ipek Williamson and her son, Jonathan, at Kempsford Manor.

arms of Sir Gilbert East over the front door, but no one seems to know who lived here during Victorian times.

I was told that during the war anything that happened at Kempsford happened at the Manor. A Major Bryant (of Bryant and May connection) lived here – maybe it was from his connection with timber the wood panelling was done. Apparently, there was stabling at that time for sixteen horses. Our gardener, Matt Cleaver, who was born in 1900, told me that cricket had been played here – so we decided that this is what the village must do. Jack Harvey came and we arranged for the cricket club to be centred here again.

I love the place so much, and I'm sure that the ethos of the house reflects all the love and work I have expended on it; it is much happier and prettier. I am proud of it and very happy for others to share the pleasure of the snowdrops and aconites and crocus in the springtime. When the garden looks particularly nice in the summer, I ask our vicar to announce it in church that the villagers are welcome to walk round. I think this is how it should be – and indeed, used to be – before people started shutting themselves away in big houses behind high fences. We have hosted a number of fund-raising concerts and fêtes here and there is a lot of interest shown in my new venture into offering it as a venue for wedding receptions. I am working on plans for short residential courses, and the Butlers' School, which was inaugurated by Lady Apsley and had such wide press coverage, is starting up again under a new tutor. There is a renewed interest in the finer points of etiquette – and it is so nice to think that it has not all been consigned to the history books.

Peggy Cooper (on the right) with her sister, Janet.

Kempsford is reputed to be one of the most haunted villages in England: I am not susceptible to seeing ghosts of humans, but I do see ghosts of dogs – perhaps that is because they are my great love. Jonathan, my son, however, will not sleep in one of the bedrooms – he says he feels the presence of an elderly man, which is very disturbing, although it is quite fashionable to boast a ghost, I suppose. When we first moved here I used to hear low voices in conversation coming from a room above me; they seemed rather sad voices. This went on for about ten years, then they stopped. We have had lots

of fun here as a family – such pleasure, and I like to think that this has now permeated the very fabric of the house.

Ipek Williamson

One Up, Two Down

Home to me when I was a toddler was the little toll-house on Ha'penny Pike Bridge. The middle of the bridge is the boundary line between Gloucestershire and Wiltshire. I was christened Margaret Doris Esme but have always been called Peggy. My dad bought the toll-house when he was first married for £50. The tolls had been done away with for years, of course. From the bridge you went straight into the living room, about ten feet by twelve, it had a tiny fireplace. Behind the door on the right was a sort of trap door with *tallet* steps down to the first bedroom. Then there was a set of ladder-like steps down to the second bedroom – the river was about halfway up the wall of that one and the water would lap and swish about just under the windowsill. The toilet was down in the garden by the big boathouse, high and dry all the year round with a cherry tree by the door and a lovely rockery covered with mauve aubretia and snow-on-the-mountain in the spring. There was also a small bush rose, called Seven Sisters. It had seven snow-white flat roses on a spray. It had grown from a sprig taken from my gran's garden in Thames Street. When we moved from the small toll-house as our family increased we took a cutting to Bridge House. My sister, Janet, took a sprig to Scotland and sent me three pieces from her bush, which I planted in a pot – it is still going strong, so that is a hundred years of old rose tales, isn't it!

The Thames played a big part in our lives. My dad was a postman at Lechlade but he also hired out boats. Behind the blackthorn hedge were dug out steps to the boathouse. We had an old green fisherman's boat that was 6d an hour and two beautiful mahogany punts with green velvet cushions. I could handle a boat when I was just seven years old, but I couldn't manage the punt pole until I was twelve. I used to row or paddle people up to St John's Lock and back, if they couldn't do it themselves, that was 6d for me for the hour, and a shilling for my dad for the hire. We also had a single scull, two double sculls and two canoes. My dad gave me a red canoe when I was fourteen, he called it *Cheemaw* after Hiawatha's canoes. There was a bus every hour from Swindon on a Sunday and folks used to come just to enjoy the river, either boating or just wandering along the old donkey towpath, it was lovely.

There was a green bathing hut and diving boards for grown-ups by the first white wooden bridge. My dad was really enterprising; he mowed the paddock early in the year and started a campsite. I always stopped to read the big notice he put up: 'No Camp Fires. No Abusive Language'. I thought it was really bossy. The tents were mainly the ridge type at that time. The Boy Scouts from Swindon used to come every year – one showed me how to slip the lock on the sash window in thefront room so that I could get out at night and go swimming with them under the Ha'penny Bridge. My mum would have slaughtered me had she known, but it was just innocent fun in those days. I think not so innocent were a few of the campers – a handful of naughty boys, and a couple of naughty Americans. One day a vicar came looking for his wife. My mum was most embarrassed and told him to look around. He did find her, from two pairs of feet sticking out of the tent door. She was dragged out and bundled off in the Reverend's car.

Up by the old Thames and Severn Canal Bridge, by the Round House, it was a picture with pink orchids and cowslips and wild blue geraniums. Fritillaries grew wild in the riverside fields, vetch – mauve and pink and yellow, moon daisies and ragged robin and quaking oats grasses. Opposite the Round House at the wooden bridge is where the Coln joins the Thames. That was icy cold – quite different where the waters meet. It made you shiver if you got in just there, the water was as clear as a bell with yellow gravel on the bottom so you could see the trout. There were lots of water voles and dabchicks and the most lovely pink flowers and water lilies and king cups – or water bubbles as some people called them. One summer, I must have been seven or eight at the time, the great painter, Augustus John, stayed with

Granny and Grampy Cooper – an old bargee.

23

Round House and Locks on the Thames at Lechlade.

The Round House and locks on the Thames at Lechlade.

us. We went for walks up to the Round House and he carried me on his shoulders over the fields to the ancient church at Inglesham. The Coopers are recorded in the Inglesham Baptismal Records as far back as 1775 – when the family was recorded as farmers and graziers. I have been told that a painting of me by Augustus John was in the National Gallery at one time.

Peggy Cooper

When Home Was A Castle

I was the sixth in a family of seven, all born at Hatherop Castle, delivered at home by Blockey – as we affectionately referred to Dr Charles Bloxsome. My mother was a widow with five children before she married my father, Francis Cadogan, he was from the family after whom Cadogan

Square in London is named. Both my mother's family and her first husband's family were strict teetotallers and that is why there was never a public house opened in the village of Hatherop.

The nursery was on the top floor and there were always two governesses: one English and the other either French or German. We had to stick to a proper school-time day and my mother – quite go-ahead for the time, I think – had the idea of having one or two children of contemporary age to her Bazley and Cadogan family to join us, and started an Ambleside School, she was a great advocate of the *PNEU* system. It was a good way to make use of a very large house, especially as my father, who was a naval man, was away a great deal. Probably, though, she did get rather bored with having so many children under her care, and Mrs Fyffe took on the school. I later went to her school at Cambridge and had the benefit of the university there. Although my home was closer to Oxford, twenty-eight miles was still considered a long way off in my youth!

We had two or three resident teachers, but it was normal for all the staff to live in. It made for a huge household as there were three in each department: the kitchen, the parlour, the pantry – presided over by Mr Barnet, the butler; the nursery – under the charge of Mrs Taylor, a wonderful old nanny who became housekeeper. There were even three Aga cookers, set side by side in the huge kitchen to cope with the enormous amount of meals. My mother was the first lady in the area to dispense with the traditional footmen – she had parlour maids instead – but Williamstrip Park retained their footmen. I remember how smart the housemaids were in their white print dresses, everyone took a pride in their appearance,

and the entire staff joined the family in the drawing-room for morning prayers, conducted by my father when he was home, otherwise it would be my mother.

I had a very happy childhood, there seemed to be a constant huge party in the house: my mother had forty-one first cousins and relatives living abroad came to the castle for their holidays, so we had lots of company. I really lived for my ponies – I used to ride a lot and would demand the groom to buy me sweets, he probably got them from the village post office. We also kept pet rabbits and guinea pigs on the front lawn, and I remember having to get up early as all our animals had to be fed before morning assembly. My cousin and I discovered that guinea pigs are quite prolific at breeding and that became a rather lucrative sideline for us, as we would sell them for what seemed to us a

Shooting party at Hatherop Castle: sitting centre are Cdr and Mrs Cadogan, with Sir Thomas Bazley standing between them – fourth to left of him is Henriette Abel Smith.

minor fortune to Harrod's, sending them off in proper crates to go by train from Fairford Station.

I also discovered that if I climbed to the top tower my very dear childhood friend, Michael Hicks-Beach, who lived at Coln Manor, could send secret signals to each other – our nannies were wonderful go-betweens. I don't think any of us children were aware that the castle was anything other than a large house which was just our home – I know I was certainly more impressed with Thornbury Castle, my mother's family home – that really has the feeling of antiquity. As children, we were intrigued by the story of Lord Derwentwater who lost his head on Tower Hill for supporting the Pretender. The lady in white who haunts the old Yew Walk is reputed to be that of his wife, Anna Maria, – the daughter of Sir John Webb, 5th Baronet, who owned the castle at the time – and certainly we never went down there after dusk, it was very spooky. There was also one passage where the dogs hated to go; their bristles would literally stand on end if they were taken down there.

Hatherop Castle was taken over during the last war for secret service training by the SOE (Special Operations Executive). We were not allowed anywhere near it which was most infuriating, although my sister Rachel and I would try to investigate strange shooting noises from the comparative safety of the wood above the river. On reflection I do think it is interesting that my old childhood home, which has been the scene of so many changes over the centuries, is now a well-known school on a scale which my mother could not have envisaged when she first introduced proper classroom teaching for her own family.

Henriette Abel Smith

Hatherop Castle Hauntings

Hatherop Castle boasts several ghosts, according to a letter written in 1899 to the daughter of Sir Thomas Sebastian Bazley, who was my great-grandfather. There is mention of strange lights and nocturnal noises in the Tapestry Room, and of a figure in the Blue Room who 'came to comfortably tuck you up in bed, but as fast as you looked one side, it invariably was on the other'. There were sliding panels, and odd corners and passages, no doubt leading to the subterranean passage of a mile long which led out into a granary – so a famous place for plots and conspiracies of those days. The story goes that the Earl of Derwentwater escaped from a chamber closet over the North Porch, which for years was untouched. Charles I and Henrietta Maria are said to have held Court in the long black oak room – so, altogether, a home with a long and interesting history.

My great-grandfather, according to a newspaper report on his death, was also a most interesting person: a great philanthropist and enormous benefactor to the estate, which he managed himself. He was a keen astronomer and wrote a number of works on the subject, he was also talented in such varied fields as gardening, handicrafts and music. It was this Sir Thomas who planted the great acreage of woodland, including Macaroni Woods on the estate, but a lot of woods was felled for the timber needed in the Great War. Apparently, he made quite an impression cycling on what was described at the time as 'a machine of curious pattern – a unique type of cycling mechanism'.

Susan Vicary

Sir Thomas Sebastian Bazley on his unique cycling machine, c. 1910

In House And Home

Our poor gran. I shall never forget the washing, it was washing everywhere when I was a child in Granny Agg's house. Everyone called her Granny, never Mrs Agg – she was just like a real granny to everyone. She was left a widow at a very early age and had to take in washing to get enough money to keep the family. As well as Dr Bloxsome's, she did Miss Crook's and Mr Parker's – they lived in the Park Villas at the end of Park Street where we lived. I had to go up and down to collect and deliver it. Another of my jobs was after I came back from Sunday school I had to change out of my best clothes and go up into the back shed with empty sugar boxes and with my little shovel I had to fill them so far up with the coal slack, then add just the right amount of water to bind it together. That set overnight to make a sort of block of coal which Gran could keep the copper fire going with on the Monday.

There was no washing powder, just soda and bar soap. There were three huge tin baths hanging on the back wall; one for washing, one for clear water for rinsing and one for the blue bath – there was always a blue bag around. Then she made the starch in another bowl, mixing the powder with boiling water because the men's shirt collars and cuffs and all the table linen and that sort of thing were starched. I can see her now turning over the heavy wooden lid from the top of the copper to lay the clothes on the smooth side to rub the soap on and scrub the clothes. She was always cheerful and always made time for everyone and anyone who called – and there was always someone from the street calling in for a cup of tea, to borrow half a cup of sugar, or a screw of tea – which she would give to them with a smile, no matter how little we had for ourselves – and a sympathetic ear or motherly advice.

My mother was a real hard worker, too. She was housemaid for the Bloxsome family until Dr Harold died. She later cleaned the Hilary Cottage Surgery when it was up Coronation Street, getting up early to finish it before the doctors opened up in the morning, then she would bike down the Mill Lane to do the police station.

Peggy Corso

Dot Jefferies 'doing' the police station front step.

Catch Lodge Caught Up In Wartime

My mother, Annie Lawrence, was born at Spring Cottage at West End Gardens and met my father while she was in service in Chelsea. At the outbreak of war she wanted to come back to Fairford so we moved down here in to her old family home. My father joined us shortly afterwards, due to health reasons, so at least we were all together and out of the London bombing. It was more like an encampment, but somehow we all squeezed in to the cottage. There was a blanket hung across on a wire to separate my bed from the grown-ups'.

After a spell in a cottage at Norman's farm at Horcott, we moved across the fields between Totterdown and Kempsford to the old gamekeeper's cottage, called Catch Lodge. Over the years the name got corrupted to Cat's Lodge, it was right on the edge of Catch Lodge Woods and my father rented it from Charles Rickards, but Maj. Northern had the shooting rights in the woods. It was a squarish house with a very deep sloping back roof that came down to the first floor and was originally two cottages. It was quite primitive – the old earth closet had two wooden seats side by side, one smaller and lower than the other, that was for the children – but it was stone-built and attached to the house, whereas most cottages at that time had their privy right up the garden.

It was ideal for us – a family of boys – we had great fun in the woods and had a number of dens, sometimes we would take out our airguns and have our own target practice. Catching rabbits for dinner was just so easy then, and the mainstay of many families during the war years. We also kept a lot of chickens and ducks, so we were well fed,

although Dad, being a Londoner, hadn't any idea or nerve about killing them. I remember the foreman of the Irish workforce that had started on what was fast becoming the RAF base offered to do it and made really short work of it, much to my horror at the time.

I had only just started school when we first went to Catch Lodge, it was a very long walk but my brothers and I soon found a short cut through Broad Ground Wood and into Totterdown Lane. The road from the lodge to the Whelford-Kempsford road was very wide. It was an ancient drove road to Avebury. The locals used to tell my father that the lodge was built over a centuries-old footpath and if they cared to exercise their rights they could walk right through the house. They didn't while we were there, but

Queueing for water at Gassons Road, Lechlade, during a drought in the seventies. The gardens here had been under water only a few months earlier in the winter floods.

it was an established public footpath and it was not unusual for families on their traditional Sunday walk to use the garden path.

Work on the base started in 1942 and my father worked in the Department of Environment. There was a large Irish workforce, my mother used to make tea for them and a couple of the workers lodged with us for a while. The main contingent lived in the Nissen huts down the hill, where Faulkner's Close is now. Work was going on all around us, the woods next to us were felled as they were right in the path of the intended runway – we were next to be moved out of the way. A network of steel cables was fastened round the cottage, rather like tying up a parcel with string, and as we set off on the lorry with our belongings to move to Vines Row the great hawser pulled and reduced Catch Lodge to rubble – the home of generations of gamekeepers, built on the ancient public right of way, was no more. Just a memory of an idyllic boyhood period for my brothers and me, learning the joys of the countryside.

Terry Keene

Floods

The first year of the new Millennium will certainly be remembered as the year of the floods. We had seen old photos of flooding in Milton Street before the main drainage was put in, but this is the first time in living memory that this cottage in Waterloo Lane has been flooded. It is the lowest lying cottage in the street, but quite a distance from the river. It is also the oldest in this immediate vicinity, appearing as the only one standing end on to the road in Kip's engraving. We expected the ditch in front that takes the water from the Green to overflow,

but it didn't; the water came in a rush through the back door and bubbled up through the carpet in the dining room. There was 10in of water in that room and 6in in the kitchen. The worst thing about this kind of flooding is, of course, that the drains just couldn't take the volume so as neighbours who have suffered these effects will tell you, it is the sewage and waste water which comes with it that is so awful.

Julian has a collection of some 7,500 books, mainly in his downstairs study – a huge number of them have been badly damaged. It was impossible to get everything off the floor, so all the electrical equipment was completely ruined. I have been storing things like milk and dairy products in bags on the back doorstep ever since and we are forced to live upstairs until the work is finished. The whole ground floor has had to be stripped. The walls are some 2ft 6in thick – it is like having the history of the two cottages that have become this one peeled away, layer after layer to the original stone shell.

Sonia McDermott

The Joneses At The Hall

The Walter Jones were my grandparents. They moved to Morgan Hall soon after Edwin Abbey left. Eileen, their eldest daughter, was born at Lechlade Manor but Margaret, Daphne and Ruth – my mother – were all born at Morgan Hall, and it was to the Hall that we came first to Fairford when my parents returned from Rhodesia, so I was brought up in the old tradition of having a nanny – she was simply part of the family, as was everyone who worked there.

My first lessons were at Miss Chew's small school. She was a brilliant teacher and

Milton Street. Fairford, 1921. Children taken to school by lorry through the flood.

The year 2000: floods again. New houses replace Townsend's garage, houses and Busby's garage seen in the previous picture.

Sonia and Julian McDermott show Joss Barker the stripped walls of their cottage, which was severely damaged in the Millennium floods.

taught me to read at an incredibly early age. My parents always attributed my later academic success to Miss Chew. I remember that I had great difficulty with adding up, and she wouldn't allow me to go home until I learnt the numbers of the coloured counters. She was a kindly disciplinarian. I was terrified of Miss Long at my next small school, so I really looked forward to the sight of her getting out the mats and placing them on the floor for our after lunch nap!

After we had moved away, the return to Morgan Hall was like returning home, and we would all spill out of the car – family, dog, cat and goldfish – at every opportunity. Granny was very independent and was determined from the outset that she would pay her way and kept very detailed accounts of her

dairy and kitchen garden that seemed to be always dripping with fruit. One great treat was for us to watch Mr Barnfield milk one of the Jerseys straight into our Peter Rabbit mugs, creamy, still warm and frothy – it was wonderful, but if we were naughty he would squirt us instead. I loved to go down to the river just as dawn was breaking, and several times Simon and I would go down to the station, catch the train to Lechlade, buy a morning paper and come back on the next train. We had a special treat once when the driver let us ride in the cab with him.

My grandmother was closely involved in everything going on in the community – the hospital, the WI, the Church, Guides, Red Cross – she saw it as an obligation for families such as she came from to help those who were not so privileged, but never in a patronizing way, just simply taking part. In the same way everyone who worked at Morgan Hall was regarded as an integral part of the family: Nan – Nanny Ethel – Waters, Barnie, and Eva Bailey – I loved Eva, her son Doug and my mother were practically brought up together and were the greatest of friends. Granny insisted that we always kept in touch with everyone. She certainly instilled in her daughters a great care for the community even though they had been packed off to boarding school at the earliest age possible after being released from nanny's apron strings.

Aunt Daphne was ten when my mother was born and this is the little letter she wrote to her:

'Langford Grange
Nr Lechlade, Glos

My dear Baby

I hope you are very well. Have you thought up a name for yourself yet. If you have I hope it is a nice one. Miss Heathcot said she saw you looking out of the window when we passed yesterday. I am writing in this writing cause I think it will be easer for you to read. I expet Nurse will read it to you if you cant. I don't think you have begun lessons yet. I shell see you on Saturday can you make your dog bark yet. We went to tee with Shela Delmis yesterday. From Daphne.'

My mother was passionate about wild flowers – the field beyond the garden was full

Margaret, Daphne and Nan Jones haymaking at Morgan Hall, c. 1919.

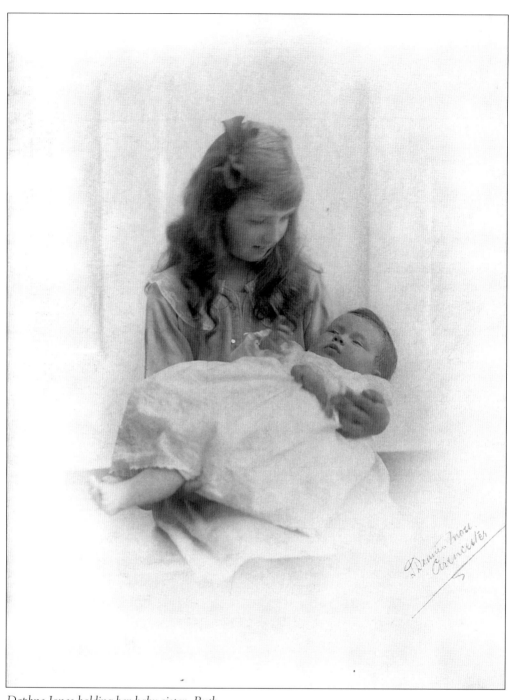

Daphne Jones holding her baby sister, Ruth.

of primroses and cowslips in the springtime, and there was a huge colony of fritillaries in the water meadow which is now the lake beyond the old railway engine yard. There were so many flowers, we just took them all for granted and picked them by what seemed the armful – but Mother always got me to draw them and identify them. Likewise with birds' eggs – we didn't realize at that time they would ever be in need of protection. My abiding picture of my mother was like some old painting of a sun-hatted lady flitting among the flowers with a butterfly net. She did a lot of work for the Gloucestershire Trust for Nature Conservation and went on numerous field trips 'botanizing' as she put it. One of her last and most comprehensive projects was to catalogue every living plant at Whelford Pools and the whole stretch of Ernest Cook land from Lea Wood to the river and down to the Mill.

Daphne and Margaret quietly rebelled against their privileged background. They could not escape academically to make their mark in a profession such as medicine or law, so they went into nursing – and this became more a pioneering dedication: Margaret went abroad as a missionary nurse; Daphne devoted most of her life to the East End – a world apart from the society into which she was born. I remember once passing some grand Cotswold manor with her and she just let slip quite casually that it was where she used to go for dancing lessons with the Mitford girls. But, in the same way, my mother never made anything of the fact that one of her godmothers was Mrs Neville Chamberlain – I think, if anything, she regarded her as being rather lacking in her spiritual duty towards her as a child.

Daphne was certainly one of the most memorable characters of the community. She was extremely fond of animals and I think made a bit of a nuisance of herself at the end of evening service because she wouldn't allow the church to be locked up until Tiddles the church cat had been accounted for. It was Daphne's last instruction that she was to be buried behind Tiddles. She is. Diana Lee-Browne, who carved Dorothy Keble's memorial stone, is carving a circular one to mark her resting spot.

Susan McGill

CHAPTER 3

Working Life

Nelson Lane: the last coachman at The Bull Hotel.

The Last Coachman

My father, Nelson Lane, was the last coachman at The Bull. He looked after the horses there all his life in the days when Hugh Busby's father owned it. My dad drove the mail coach into Cirencester as well as meeting the guests at the railway station and bringing them and their luggage to the hotel. Sometimes he would take us children with him in one of the horse buses up to Millie Davis at The Carriers Arms at Horcott. We thought that was wonderful and we got lovely fresh vegetables from Mr Davis who had a big allotment behind the pub – he was the husband of Nurse Davis, the district nurse, and brother to the landlord.

On Boxing Day when the Meet was held in the Market Place my dad took round the stirrup cup to the huntsmen – it was such a colourful sight, just like a picture postcard Old England, my dad looking all smart in his livery, too. He would sometimes take me with him when he took the lunch hampers down to the fishermen at the Old Bull and

Bush, the old wooden hut which belonged to The Bull. It had a very twisted May blossom bush growing by the door that was said to date back to some ancient rights of ale being sold where a bush or branch of a tree was displayed – a bit like an inn sign I suppose. There were certainly a few bottles of beer with the ham and cold beef sandwiches in the wicker hampers.

Of course, my dad was very well known to the farmers from all around when they came here on market days. If any of them had too much to drink – and a few of them did when they all met up – my dad had to drive them home. There was one horse in particular which my dad spoke about – old Sure To. When that farmer was a bit too merry to drive, my dad could drop the reins and Sure To really lived up to his name, because he was sure to find his way back to the farm.

One of Dad's other jobs was to help with catching the pike – they had to be cleared every so often because they ate the trout, and that was what The Bull was famous for, its trout fishing. This was how he lost his life. He must have leant over from the river bank with this long pole with a ring at the end and fallen in head first. I was only seven when he died, the youngest of us five girls. There were no horses at The Bull after that time. He lived for his horses and died on his job in the Coln meadow where they had grazed for so long.

Dora Thompson

Ten Shillings A Month For Mother

My mother used to tell me I was born at 'The Back of Beyond' and I thought that was the proper name for the cottage tucked back from the main road near Warren's Cross until I learnt to read, to discover the name was really Trout House.

One day when I came home from school I was told to have a quick bath in the old tin tub, I was then bundled into a second-hand print frock, a quick rake through my hair and Gran's big black hat, which served her for Sundays and funerals and chapel bun-fights, was jammed on top. Mother then gave me a brown paper parcel and told me there was a change of knickers, petticoat and black stockings in it, uniform 'was provided'. She walked with me between the brooks and handed me over to the cook at the back door. I was 'in service' within an hour of leaving school. I was just thirteen, but had passed the Fourth Standard – which was the qualification for leaving school – and I didn't get a half-day off for a month.

My mother and my sisters moved away, but I stayed and after a few years I got a job at Ryton House. I worked for the cook-house-keeper, she was the queen bee and ruled the lives of the kitchen maid and scullery maid. I had to be up and ready for work at six o'clock in the morning and didn't finish until ten at night. My wages were 10s a month 'with all found', that meant my uniform, a bedroom which I had to share with one of the housemaids, and meals – more often than not that would be only what was left over from the dining room – and that 10s I had to send home to Mother. My father had dropped down dead at work in the field when I was just eight years old, the eldest of four children, and there was no financial support in those days. My mother was so proud she would not have gone 'to the parish' for any help.

I had a half-day off each week – well, that turned out to be three o'clock in the afternoon before I could get out of my uniform and I had to be back in the house by 6.30

Esther Nash at the seaside with her Aunt Esther in the early thirties.

p.m. I couldn't possibly get home in those couple of hours, so I went to my Aunt Esther's at Spring Gardens. Her husband, Uncle John Ryman drove the horse-drawn coach to and from the railway station for The New Inn. Aunt Esther was my father's sister and I was named after her so I hated my name as she was such an old tyrant, but she did have a very nice young man lodging with her, James Lewis, he had a wonderful smile and was a very popular figure in Stroud's shop – the County Stores. When we got married he always called me Ettie. Perhaps he didn't want to be reminded about Aunt Esther – especially as one day while we were there Mr Constable came to her house and she set about him with her brolly for putting up the rent!

Esther Nash

Donkey Cart to Fairford Flyer

I was born in Number 3 Mill Lane Cottages, long since demolished, one of the youngest of a family of ten. We later moved to Milton Place, known to us locals as Tiger's Bay! I left school at fourteen to work as 'groom' to the donkey belonging to the Misses Keble, relatives to the famous Revd John Keble, the Poet Divine, who started the Oxford Movement. I first had to catch the donkey then get it harnessed to the cart and bring it round to the front door of Keble House, ready for Miss Janet and Miss Grace to go visiting. My wages then, in 1915, were 6s a week.

In 1917 I became a cleaner on the railway in South Wales. One foolish trick of ours was to find an engine 'in the field' (an outside siding) and crawl into the firebox for warmth. We were unlucky one day to be

Mill Lane Cottages, 1966 – now demolished.

Fairford railway staff. Ted Law is seventh from the left.

found by the foreman cleaner and sent home for the day – with our pay docked, of course. We were getting £1 a week at this time for sixty hours' work.

I returned to Fairford in 1919 as fireman and did twenty years' service at that grade and became a driver with short spells on other lines during the war, spending several uncomfortable hours in various tunnels in the Birmingham district dodging the wrath of German bomber crews. Once back at Fairford as 'top link' driver, I stayed until May 1962, when I had completed forty-five years' service. I was presented with my gold watch in recognition of my long service to the railway and my redundancy notice a few weeks later when the Fairford branch closed on 16 June 1962.

Ted Law

Lechlade Railway

It was only a few days after I had finished my schooling that Mother said, 'Mr Boulter wants you to start work in the station office'. I was to replace Frank Sparkes who had left to join the RAF. I had rather grand visions of the job and was quite disillusioned when I saw how poky the office was, and really draughty. It was in the middle of wartime and the railways were extremely busy, especially for the first morning train which took many women from Lechlade to Witney to work in the munitions and blanket factories. The workmen's ticket, as it was called for this journey, was 11d. My first wage was 19s 7d and Frank Boulter, the stationmaster, who was my boss, would say, 'I'll toss you for it

– if I win you will get 19s 6d; if you win I'll give you £1'. He was a real dyed in the wool railway man, and took a great pride in his job. I soon learned to work even more carefully on market days when he had met his friends for a lunchtime drink. He had a booming bass voice, which he used to great effect on the job and in the church choir.

I taught myself to type on the ancient Remington but there was also a lot of ledger work: separate invoices had to be raised for passengers and goods and they had to be balanced every month. Then there were the credit accounts for the farmers using the railway lorries to collect the corn to be transported. I was responsible for booking special horseboxes for the valuable brood mares sent from Mr and Mrs Honour at

Eastleach to Ireland. Occasionally there would be a pig in a crate – that travelled in the guard's van. There was also the country lorry service for delivering parcels to the villages each week.

As the workload increased, on top of booking trains, issuing tickets and cashing up, Peggy Cooper was taken on to work alongside me. Later on, Enid Hicks joined us. We used to scrounge some coal from the engine drivers for the little open fireplace. We had to help on occasion with the station garden, that was a great source of pride on the railways but we were not allowed to clip the box hedges or even attempt the topiary. It was certainly colourful with flowers and we were proud that Lechlade won a couple of prizes.

Lechlade station.

It was the custom at that time that when someone from the railway got married, Early's would present them with a pair of their Witney blankets – valued then at £7 10s. I still have the ones they gave to Ted and me when we married in 1950.

Beryl Law

Middle Clerk

I enjoyed my job in the GWR office, except for Saturday afternoons because that was when Beryl, being the senior clerk, had her half-day off. I usually had Wednesdays and it nearly always rained. I can still remember the names – and the wages – of the railway staff at Lechlade 1946-47. The wages sheet was headed by Mr Boulter, because he was the stationmaster and earned the most: £5 a week, then came Jack Thornton, Mr Mann and Jack Hunt, drivers; Derek Musty, lorry driver, Mr Pettifer, porter, Mr Pratley and Mr King, signalmen, Imbert Scarrott – he was just listed as 'boy'. Mr Bulley was the crossing keeper and Mrs Selina Bulley did one afternoon duty for which she was paid 2s. Some of the lorry drivers did portering as well. Then there was Beryl who earned £1 more than me because she was head clerk, and Enid Hicks, who had 5s less than me because she was third clerk.

I was pleased to have the office job at the station – especially as my Mum had other plans for me as soon as I left school. I had come home from school on a Friday teatime, two weeks after my fourteenth birthday, to find old Florence in our kitchen. She was the housemaid from General Fawkes's house at Riverside. 'So,' says Mum, 'You have left school then. Now on Monday you will be at Mr Fawkes's house at 7 a.m. to help Florence in the kitchen. There'll be the cleaning, get

Mary Anne Morse at Little Faringdon level crossing, c. 1915.

42

Lechlade post office staff, 1911. Mrs Sadler the postmistress (wearing hat) stands centre.

breakfast, wash up, get lunch, wash up then you can come home from two o'clock till four, but you have to be back to work until dinner is finished and you've washed up.' Utter silence. 'No, I will not – I'll never work in that house – never.' Well, I had my ears boxed for that and I was sent to bed for the rest of the day with her words ringing in my head: 'You will get up early tomorrow and get on your bike and don't come back until you've got a job.'

I went all round Lechlade looking for a job, then I asked Miss Parrot at the post office where my Dad was postman. 'Try the Wessex Nurseries,' she said, 'they want a girl.' So off I went as fast as my bike would take me and was so relieved when old Mr Dumbleton said he would take me on to work in the packing shed and greenhouses with the carnations and tomatoes. I started at 7.15 a.m. and fin-ished at 5.15 p.m., with a ten-minute break in the morning and half an hour for lunch, which wasn't time to get home so I took a packet of sandwiches and a drink of water. My school friend Eva worked there too, so that made it happier. At noon on the Saturday we stood in line for our wages: I had 16s 4d. I bought my Mum a bunch of carna-tions – seconds, which cost 6d. When I gave them to her, she asked how much wages I had: 'Give me the 10s,' she said, 'you can have the 6s 4d'. After a few weeks, though, my dad took me down to Barclays Bank and opened an account for me with half a crown. I still have that money box – the key was handed over to me a few years ago as a keep-sake as it was the only money box still in use at the bank.

Peggy Cooper

Park House, Fairford, c. 1920.

Maid Above Stairs

I was housemaid at Park House for Colonel and Mrs Palmer. He was the Palmer side of the Huntley and Palmer biscuit firm – I understand his was the side that developed the recipes and the know-how. Park House was what would be called the Manor House of Fairford, set in beautiful parkland. There were twenty-five bedrooms – the top storey was the servants' quarters. There was over a dozen of us staff looking after just Colonel and Mrs Palmer. Mrs Palmer had a lady's maid, Miss Hood – she's up in the church-yard now of course, and the Colonel had his valet, who was also one of the two chauffeurs. There was a butler, footman and hall boy – they all waited at table among their other

jobs. The hall boy had to keep all the open fires and the boiler in the cellar going. I was head housemaid over two under maids and I was responsible for the linen cupboard as well. We only had one vacuum cleaner between us, but plenty of dustpans and brushes. The men cleaned all the silver and brass. Mr Derry was head gardener and my dad, Bill Winstone, was under him, then there were six more men in the gardens sup-plying all the food for the house, the large staff and a great many visitors.

The Colonel had two cars and travelled a lot to Cheltenham – he was a JP and was put forward to be knighted but he didn't want to be a Sir. His brother was Sir Eric Palmer, his daughter was Dila Palmer, an actress, but I don't remember her ever coming to the Park.

Nancy Jones (on right), aged eight, with her sister, Doris, aged five.

But David Niven did. He was such a nice man. So easy to look after and ever so handsome, but not a bit haughty although he was such a famous film star. He was Colonel Palmer's godson and made quite a stir when he judged at the carnival with Mrs Gordon Lennox, the daughter of Sir Lionel Darrell, she was also the Palmers' godchild. She inherited all the linen; beautiful it was, all embroidered with a palm tree monogram to represent the name Palmer. The men's uniform had silver buttons with the emblem on them – they were very smart. We had to provide our own uniform, my granny made my first dresses: blue cotton for the morning with white apron and cap; black for the afternoon with a short fancy apron and I had to slip on cuffs which were stiff and washable to keep my sleeves clean. When the lady's maid died I mainly looked after the mistress and her pet pekinese, Boys. The electricity for the house was generated at the Mill. Bill Brindle's grandfather looked after the turbine. The private carriageway from Park House to the railway station was down Lovers Walk and the old pillars to the gateway are still there.

The Palmers used to go away each year for about five weeks while we spring-cleaned the house – there were a lot of rooms to do: an impressive front hall, a lovely dining room and a big library which had a false bookcase on one wall concealing a door that led to the hall. The long window in the north hall looked right over the Deer Park where the American Hospital was built during the war and up to the obelisk. The smoking parlour was oak panelled and decorated all in brown so as not to show the smoke. There was also a billiard room, and the bothy – that was where the hall boy cleaned all the boots and shoes. Both Colonel and Mrs Palmer hunted. It was a splendid sight when we had the opening meet at the Park – the red coats and everyone looking so smart on beautiful horses, and the silver trays filled with glasses of sherry all sparkling in the sunlight as they were handed round by the footmen. There was a fine set of tennis courts, one was an all-weather court, there were always a lot of guests throughout the year so it wasn't just two people in that big place all the time. They also made sure that we enjoyed ourselves, too. Every year they gave us a staff ball and we could invite the staff from Hatherop Castle and Stowell Park, then we were invited back to theirs in turn.

When Harry, one of the footmen, and I started having our alternate Sundays off together and walking out we knew that if we got married we would have to leave because living-in situations and married couples, especially of they were of the age to start a family, were not allowed. Anyway, we decided to get married and when Mrs Palmer heard about it she sent for me, I went to her room knowing that she would tell me I had to leave. But what she did say nearly bowled me over.

'Nancy,' she said, 'I hear you are getting married. I shall pay for all your wedding clothes and the Colonel wishes you to have your reception here and he will pay for it.' I was able to have eighty guests – family and friends. The head cook and her team did all the food, except for the wedding cake. Colonel Palmer had that made at Huntley and Palmer's to the same recipe as theirs had been. Then I was driven to Swindon with my three bridesmaids – my sister, Irene, my niece, June Kilminster, and one of the housemaids, Doris Radway – Mulcock as she was then. We thought we were royalty – chauffeur driven in the Colonel's car. We went to McIlroys and chose a beautiful white gown for me and my bridesmaids were in pink.

I was let loose in the lovely gardens to pick

Nancy Jones at her wedding to Harry Bartlett on the north terrace of Park House.

whatever I needed for our bouquets, which I made myself. On the day, the last of August 1938 it was, the chauffeur collected my dad from the Mill then came up the Park for me. Lady Darlington from East End House came up to dress me. Oh my! I was really the lady of the manor that day. The Colonel and Mrs Palmer came to the service at St Mary's church, but they slipped away quietly afterwards and left Harry and me with our guests to have the run of the house for the wedding feast.

Colonel Palmer died the year after we got married, Harry and I left, of course. I had my son, David, two years later and Carole came along a few years after that, but I went back to help out when Mrs Palmer needed me. Then the war broke out and Park House and all its grounds were taken over by the military. Mrs Palmer went up to Burdocks House for a while until she died. The lovely old

house was pulled down in the 1950s, it had got into a bad state during the troop occupation, and the new Farmor's School was built on its site. It really was the end of a long chapter – and a way of life such as we shall never see again, and to think that in all those hundreds of years that the mansion stood there I was the last to be married from there – and me the housemaid at the time.

Nancy Jones

The Daily Round

My working day started before daybreak for almost forty years. I have just retired from the post round after twenty years, delivering mail to 374 houses in the town area, and on many occasions, such as telephone bill times, every house had some post. I think I know every

Audrey Cowley on her milk round.

letter box by nature: the upright ones which are difficult to push open with one hand while trying to get the envelopes in with the other; the too-small ones, those with thick draught-excluder liners that push the letters back out, and the snap-quick sort that try to get your fingers and I got to know where the family dog sat ready to catch the mail.

I was born in the lodge house then we moved to the gardener's cottage in Fairford Park. My father worked for the Palmers when they had the Park House, and continued in the gardens when the estate was taken over by the Ernest Cook Trust. It was a fairly long bike ride down the driveway before I started work each morning, but I loved it, especially the summer dawn when the Park seemed to come alive with the sound of birds singing, and the rabbits and hares bobbing about in the grassland and the ducks waddling along-side the drive. There was a little owl that perched on the fence by the gate and it would turn its head to watch me pass by. Of course, cold, dark and wet early mornings were a dif-ferent story. It took a couple of hours to sort the mail and load the bicycle. Post bikes are very sturdily built to take the weight on the front and are quite distinctive. We got used to working out obscure addresses, such as 'the door but one from the fish and chip shop' – being local really helped then. Perhaps one of the most unusual pieces of mail we received was the yearly envelope marked 'the post lady of Fairford'; inside was a dried flower with a little note asking for it to be placed on the grave of Mr Hedges, the old headmaster here who died in his 100th year, the envelope also contained a toffee 'for the post lady for doing it'.

Before being a post lady I was the 'milk lady' and delivered all round Fairford with a pony and float for seventeen years. I had to start work then at 5.30 a.m. as I had to catch the pony first. I worked with three different ponies during that time – each had a will of its own. My first was Tommy, a really steady plodder, which was good as far as I was concerned as I had never worked with horses before and had to train with him, getting him to stop and start in the right places. My next was Gipsy, a black-and-white horse from the North who had worked for a rag-and-bone man. She knew which day was dustbin day and would stop and nose off the lids to have a good old scavenge inside the bins. The last was Timmy. He would delay working for as long as possible and be at the far end of the field by the river, so I had a fair walk to catch him before harnessing up. He always had the idea that the grass was greener on the other side and had the habit of moving across the road at a whim to try the grass on the opposite verge. I enjoyed working the daily round – it is something that overseas visitors comment on – it is a lovely part of our traditional life.

Audrey Cowley

One of Them or One of Us

I was always amazed how long the old social attitudes lingered in Lechlade. In the early seventies I helped my husband with his milk round, with the deliveries when necessary and collecting the money on Saturdays. One lady asked me if I would help with cleaning the church and I explained that I just didn't have the time, what with helping with the dairy work, my child to care for and, of course, my job. Raising a somewhat disinterested eyebrow she asked what my job was – I told her I was head teacher at a school in Swindon. There was a visible change in her

attitude, and it became more noticeable as word got around. Instead of being announced as 'the milk woman' when I knocked on the doors I was variously invited to 'just open the door, my dear, the money is on the salver in the hall' and 'you must come in for a coffee'.

One of our customers, old Mrs Moss who lived in The Shrubberies, never changed. I think I probably gave her more back in cigarettes than she gave me in milk money – but she had smoked since she was seven years old, so she saw no reason to change her habit of a lifetime in later years. She was one of the last barge families of the Thames. She recalled the day her father brought in three clay pipes: 'one for him, one for my Mam, and one for me – your sister's only five, so she be too young to have one,' he said. It was interesting to learn from her how the bargees' children got their education: when they were at Lechlade they collected work from the school and would take it for marking to a school in Bristol when eventually the family arrived there.

Brenda Miller

Nursery Work

Milton Street Nurseries were well established by the time Don's parents bought them in 1962 from Cyril and Aubrey Smith – no relation. They had originally been part of the Fairford manorial holdings and were given by Percy Fitzhardinge Raymond Barker to his son, Reginald, when he reached the age of twenty-one in 1896. The property and land was sold in 1923 for £550 to Harry Baum at the time when large parts of the Fairford Park estate were sold off. The nurseries covered almost an acre and had four heated greenhouses, the largest being 120ft long. When I

Don Smith at the back of the Milton Street nurseries.

married Don and came here in 1974 the old coke boiler had to be stoked twice a day. The little boiler house was down two deep steps and I have memories of helping to bale the water out each time it rained heavily. In addition to the greenhouses there was a lean-to and a potting shed, pigsties and an old donkey shed.

Don's speciality was growing tomatoes; there was never enough to satisfy local customers because they really were good, he always let them ripen on the vine. It was a big job at the end of each season to scrub all the greenhouses out with Jeyes fluid. I remember planting a hundredweight of white daffodil bulbs in three rows down the entire length of the garden and nurturing them in time for Easter. One year I picked 1,000 blooms which had to be bunched up and boxed for the Gloucestershire Market at Cheltenham, and the Fosseway Nurseries would take just as many as we could produce. There were also the bedding plants to deal with and as Christmas approached it was busy with making holly wreaths. Jan Peters let me cut as much as I liked from her magnificent tree to help out what we grew in our own gardens. I spent many a wet hour scrambling around the countryside ditches gathering moss for the frames, it was very hard work on the hands but we did like them to be completely natural and would never have put artificial flowers in them.

Because of the work at the nurseries I could only work part-time at my profession as a cook-caterer. I was at Fairford Hospital for nineteen years, and it was like cooking for a large family when put into perspective with my post as Domestic Bursar at Leicester University where I was responsible for the catering for 240 students plus staff, especially as we bought locally at that time – meat from David Perry's, fruit and veg from what we called Dessie's. That great feeling of being so much part of a community even extended to cooking the patients' favourite meals – one of the most popular being my adaptation of Rosemary Yells' liver and tomato casserole from the recipe book compiled from local favourites for the Hospital funds.

Likewise, I had shown an interest in the local Silver Band and one Sunday morning Cecil Price came round with a little case and a Tune-A-Day book and suggested I 'had a go on the cornet'. Well, I couldn't get a proper note out of it for a week – but I persevered with it in time to take part in the parade for the Queen's Silver Jubilee, but only managed to contribute the odd note, hopefully in the right place, as I found how difficult it is to play and march at the same time. That was twenty-five years ago and I have been with the Band ever since.

May Smith

Pills And Precision

My father, Harry Smith, worked as the pharmacist's assistant at Davis the Chemist from the age of fourteen until he retired. Every day at noon, when he left the shop for his lunch break, he walked across the Market Place to St Lawrence's and climbed – I think it is forty-seven – steps to wind the church clock which is in the stage between the ringing chamber and the bells. There were two weights to wind up by a crank handle. I often went with him when I was a child, and it was quite a treat for small groups of other children to see the clock wound up. It's an old

Harry Smith dispensing at Davis the chemists, Lechlade.

Harry Smith winding the clock in the church tower of St Lawrence.

clock, known as a 'four-poster', and dates back to around 1760. It's obviously not the first one to be installed in the tower.

As a Churchwarden I was interested to see in one of the old Churchwarden's accounts of 1558 an entry relating to an agreement with a Christopher Bellyngham that, for a yearly fee of 1s that 'he do come and looke to The Clocke to mend hym yf need so require'. My father wound the clock from the thirties, except for the war years when he was serving overseas, right until 1974 when it was electrified – the cost was largely paid for from the legacy left by Alf King, who was such a stalwart of the church, he was Tower Captain for over forty years and a keen member of the

choir. It was so important to my father that the church clock should always be right – and it was because he would adjust it when necessary, and when the summer and winter time changes came around, he would wait until it was dark and then go up the tower to put the clock forward or backward so that people who relied on the church clock wouldn't get confused with the hour's change happening in the daylight.

I suppose the greatest change, apart from the increased house building, that has been in my lifetime in Lechlade is the volume of traffic. I can remember, as a child, we could play ball and whiptop in the road and would look up when we heard a car coming, and still had time to get on to the side. It was never a problem to cross the road – my

Harry Smith with daughter Maureen.

grandmother lived opposite The Swan and we had to walk across the road to fetch water several times a day from one of the old lion's head iron pumps which used to line the main street. There is only one of those pumps left now – that is in Little London, on what was the ancient coach road through the town. It has a preservation order on it, but unfortunately some vandal has recently removed the top.

It is nice to have roots in a place and the sense of belonging increases as one gets involved more and more in local history. I never followed in the pharmaceutical footsteps of my father, but became very involved in the accounts and telephone duties in the veterinary field of my husband. Some calls could be quite amusing. One I remember was from a lady who rang in a panic-stricken voice to say she had inadvertently taken the dog's worm pills which Chris had prescribed for her pet. I was able to advise her to contact her doctor straight away. I was pleased to see her around soon after obviously fit and well!

Maureen Baxter

Vetting Over Nine Decades

I am the third generation of Baxter vets in Lechlade. My grandfather, John Richmond Baxter – always referred to locally as J.R. – started the practice at Downington House in 1903, then my father, Jack Baxter, joined him in 1925. The practice moved to the Vicarage in Sherborne Street and then to Bridge House before the purpose-built surgery in 1964. It seems that J.R.'s risqué jokes were legion – and legendary – according to the tales I've heard from the local farmers. The river played an important part

in family life. Grandfather was secretary of the Swimming Club and summertime centred around punting and riverside picnics – and, of course, the famous Water Carnival. My aunt, Kitty Baxter, was a champion swimmer.

During the war my father carried on the practice entirely single-handed over what was, and still is, a large area. When he retired he dedicated his time and efforts to local archives. Every week he travelled down to the County Record Office, researching and transcribing the Births, Marriages and Deaths registers as well as Bishops' Transcripts from 1600. He copied out a number of the censuses by hand from 1841 and the Tithe registers. All of these are invaluable for our local archives and are being put on computer to form an historical database. He was meticulous in his cataloguing and recording, but he also loved to get involved with 'hands-on' history and joined in the local archaeological digs.

The vet has always been a figurehead in a rural community, the equivalent of an old and trusted family doctor. I mourn the passing of the age when we had – or made – time for people. Care has gone out of the window. It is most important to care for the owners as well as their animals, whether it's a number of livestock or a single domestic pet. We are currently in the midst of the foot-and-mouth epidemic; farmers are distraught, fearful of what each new day will bring. I get so angry and upset as stories of over-bearing officials treating farmers so callously come to light. One farmer, for instance, was at his gate as a car pulled up. The driver simply wound down the window, passed the farmer a sheet of paper and announced 'You're under Form D' and with no further word of explanation drove off. As it happened, the contact between that farmer's animals and the trans-

Chris Baxter holds on to one of his retirement gifts.

Lechlade Home Guard.

Fairford ATC, in front of the old cricket pavilion in Park Street, 1942.

porting of a suspected case was really quite tenuous, but the effect it had on that farming family was just as devastating. The simplest comparison between this current outbreak and the one in the sixties is that of movement. The whole system has changed so much and it is unbelievable the distances that animals now travel.

I retired from our family practice in 1993 and was then appointed a Ministry vet for four years – but have now been called out of retirement to work on this current crisis. I, too, have a personal interest in the development of this countrywide disaster because I am the proud owner of two Jersey cows – a gift from the local farming fraternity. Jezebel lived up to her name, she was reared at the Burford School Farm, and a totally different character from the second cow, Wilhelmena; we still have Willie's calf, and, of course, the rustic three-legged milking stool and bucket which were presented to me at the same time. It must be pretty unusual to have a gift drag one across a field at the end of a halter – such as Jezzie did when she was handed to me; she certainly marked my official retirement in her own down to earth way.

Chris Baxter

CHAPTER 4

Medical Matters

Dr Charles Bloxsome at the wheel of his Wolseley-Siddeley AD 668, his son, Dr Harold Bloxsome, is in the back seat. Fred Keylock, his chauffeur, is standing at the front door of Croft House, c. 1905.

Doctors Of Note

Croft House, Fairford, September 1941.

My father, Charles Harold Bloxsome, came to Fairford to join James Cornwall in 1883. The Cornwalls, father and son, had their practice at Keble House, which they rented from the Revd John Keble. The first recorded Fairford doctor was a Richard Duckett, licensed 'to practise Chirurgery' in 1697. A John Carter is listed under Physic in 1792 – described as Surgeon and

Apothecary, it is feasible that these doctors were succeeded by their sons, just as James Cornwall succeeded his father and I followed mine.

We moved into Croft House in 1893 when I was eight years old – it had been my grandmother's home. My Aunt Nell Iles lived with us, and my father also took with him his invaluable man, Fred Keylock, who was to become a great mainstay of the family for more than fifty years.

Country practice is very exacting and my father had few holidays – they interfered with his routine of living and this he found unpleasant. A fishing holiday in Ireland with a friend was terminated by a telegram which he wrote to his mother to send him, recalling him to Fairford.

The parish council thought a medical man would be very useful to have as chairman, especially as my father had shown to have new ideas. He presented a paper on the Fairford Drains, which he demonstrated to be non-existent and urged a large expenditure to remedy the defect. His paper was received politely, but his proposals were declined. He retired early from that sector of public life!

Later, he became intensely interested in motor cars – to him an interesting mode of locomotion, a means of getting from one place to another as quickly as possible, but never an absorbing delight like his horses and music. It would have been difficult to become delightfully absorbed in such of the early cars as he possessed. Fired with curiosity to see Sir Evelyn Ellis on his five horse-power Panhard when he drove through Fairford in 1895, my father rushed to the post office and endeavoured to inter-

Fairford Cottage Hospital, c. 1920. Built in 1889, it has doubled in size to a fifteen-bed community hospital, but is still the smallest hospital in Gloucestershire.

view him, with poor success as the Panhard drove off in an explosive cloud of dust. Sir Evelyn had just brought it from France to drive through England in order to be prosecuted as often as possible for not having a man walking in front with a red flag. It was not until 1903 that my father was able to buy his first car – the Locomobile, an American steam car, steered by a tiller.

The microscope was to my father in his medical life what music was to him in his private life. He taught himself bacteriology and the technique of cutting sections of tissue, making vaccines and examining and counting blood cells. I remember the hours he spent with his microscope in the smoking-room which doubled as his laboratory at Montague House in the High Street before we moved to the Croft. In 1887 he admitted to Fairford Cottage Hospital John Betterton, a journeyman butcher, aged sixty-seven who died the next day. Having examined some of the fluid from the hard, purplish-black pustules from his enormously swollen arm, my father reported the case as death from anthrax. This caused immediate alarm in the district. Attacks on his professional assessment appeared in an editorial in the *Wilts and Gloucestershire Standard* and he was vilified by the Poulton squire who owned the culprit bull, supported by a vet who signed himself as Justicia. Finally, after fierce controversy, the great authority on pathology, Mr Watson Cheyne, confirmed from the case put forward by my father and the preserved tissue, that there was no doubt that the patient had died of anthrax.

The initial operations he performed at the Cottage Hospital were carried out under Lister's carbolic spray, a machine called a donkey-engine diffusing a strong vapour of carbolic acid over the patient, surgeon and attendants. It was at this point that Dr James Cornwall retired from the theatre, leaving my father to perform the operations. Not unnaturally, my father disliked being called out in the night. He had a speaking tube fixed outside the surgery door and patients could blow through it into a whistle at his bedside. This would awake him and he would hold a conversation, of a procrastinating character, with the messenger. He said the tube was also convenient for rolling down an appropriate pill so that he did not have to answer the door and thus prolong the consultation.

H.E.B.
(From some biographical jottings on his father, C.H.B.)

Red Letter Days

As a small boy in the 1890s I had a very happy time, living in Montague House opposite the church and close to the Park where we were allowed to wander about all the year round. Good Friday seemed an especial red-letter day, appearing always a mild and lovely day associated with cawing of rooks and hot cross buns for breakfast. The buns were made at Mr Ford's bakery near the Park gates, where a superb wedding cake was displayed under a glass case. The icing was like plaster of Paris and had cracked and collapsed in places. The cake went with the business when it was transferred to Mr Plank.

Even more fascinating was Mr Powell's shop. Old Tom Powell was a qualified chemist and dispensed occasionally and doubtfully a rare prescription. His son, Charlie, was much older than me, but a great friend. He was a good businessman, launching out into exciting new 'lines', especially photography, which he said was just 'coming in', and air-guns and rook rifles, a circulating library and comic papers. Cray-fishing was one of his hobbies and I went with him with my dark lantern, bought at his shop, which burnt a fluid called Colza oil, it smelt very strong and showed a green and a red light when you pressed hard on a slide.

Charlie was in the choir and took me with him to Portsmouth on the choir trip, starting from Fairford Station at 4 a.m. and coming back exhausted twenty-four hours later. My other close friend was Gerald Loxley, the vicar's son. Gerald and I were the same age and had been christened together in St Mary's church with water from the River Jordan, especially brought home by Gerald's aunt. It was supposed to have some special virtue.

I was dragged clinging on to the apron of Emma, our maid, for my first schooling to Miss Bowl who lived in our gardener's cot-tage, next door to Croft House. She used to send to Powell's for a book to read, the subject and author being of less importance than it should be 'large print and interesting'. She instilled in me a love of reading. My 'advanced schooling' was at Mr Starkey's at Mount Pleasant House. He kept good order and taught us well. I was at first much puzzled by the Mount Pleasant School song, which we sang in various keys at the end of term: called 'Gain the Laurels', I associated it in some way with the house opposite The Bull which I knew as The Laurels.

At the age of eleven I became a boarder at Magdalen College School – one of the oldest in England. I was happy there although my heart sank when I first left home and for the first few weeks my Gloucestershire accent made me far too conspicuous to be comfortable. Magdalen

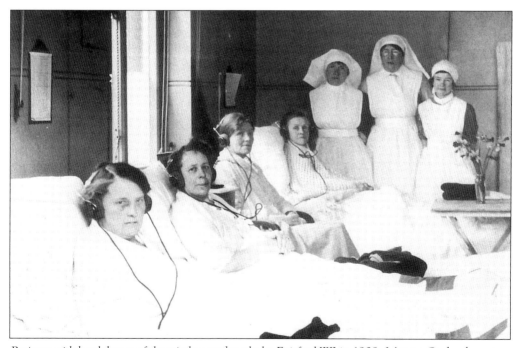

Patients with headphones of the wireless set bought by Fairford WI in 1928. Matron Orchard, centre.

Dr Harold and Mrs Bloxsome with baby daughter, Helen.

gave me the indispensable foundation and background of classics and literature for medicine. It was a choir school, and a few boys qualified for free education if they passed a very stiff trial to get into Magdalen College Choir. My mother thought we might be missing out on free education and perhaps I had a hitherto unsuspected fine voice, so she asked the headmaster's wife, Mrs Sherwood, for whom I had a great affection, to 'try my voice', which she kindly did. No, she said, she didn't think I would make it into the College Choir, nor indeed into the school's own humble choir, but she thought I might well be suited to one related post – to blow the school organ. I still look upon that kindly gesture with gratitude because I was then part of the school choir and as organ-blower joined them on their annual treats.

My mother was most affectionate and gentle. She had a great love for the Croft and its garden. She was a great gardener herself, it was her greatest pleasure, she also took up photography; developing and printing the photographs herself. She did the booking for the practice and sent out the bills, and enjoyed receipting them, often with a glass of port to the payer. She died at the age of forty-nine in 1911. There are three seats in Fairford for passers-by to rest on. They were subscribed for by the poorer people of the town, in memory of A.E.B. – my mother.

I went to St Bartholomew's Hospital at the age of seventeen, and well remember the extreme sensation of pleasure and ineffable relief when I learnt that I was at last a fully-qualified medical man, and listened entranced to one of the examiners who told us of the particular privileges our professional status carried: we should never, for the rest of our lives, be summoned to sit upon a jury and never, under any circumstances, could our horses be requisitioned for the fire engine or other parochial purpose whatever.

Dr Harold Bloxsome
(From autobiographical notes)

Cottage Hospital

I first came to Fairford Hospital as Night Sister in 1954, and found it very quiet after being a theatre nurse and working in Palestine and Iran (which was then Persia). It was the rule at that time for the night nurse to live in, but I slept at Mrs Derry's who lived in the Croft. I was then asked to take over as Assistant Matron, I was the first Sister at Fairford Hospital to be appointed to that post, although we still came under the administration of Cirencester, and I stayed until 1968.

Fairford had always been a General Practitioners' hospital under a Matron and being a small rural hospital we worked very closely with the local doctors. Although I was no longer living in I was on call during the night. I knew how difficult it was to be alone in an emergency and I was there to help when necessary with 'the last offices' as I think you can pay more respect to the job in hand when there are two of you. On occasion when I was alone on night duty if a patient had died and was too heavy for me to move I rang the police station and was very grateful for the help the policeman would give me. This was especially welcome as there was no light at that time in the little chapel of rest and it was a bit scary having to do all the moving around and find your way down the garden by the light of a hand torch. That was one example of the impor-

Sister Ruth Batty at Fairford Hospital on the opening of the sitting room replacing the old operating the-atre with Granny Johnson, sitting. From left to right: Mrs Margaret Iles, Charlie Godding, Edwin Ansell, -?-, Mrs Walter Jones, Mrs Boulton, Aubrey Smith, Mrs Dorothy Morgan, Arthur Goodman, Matron Anne McNeil, Tom Boulton.

tance of being part of a close community.

This was illustrated again when the two young doctors, Dr Shaw and Dr Veale, took over the practice. They were like a breath of fresh air to the place. The patients loved it when one Christmas Dr Shaw came dressed in a tutu, black make-up round his eyes and wearing bright red lipstick – and a pipe! Dr Veale was robed as Father Christmas and they were careering around with the trolleys distributing the presents from under the tree. Dr Veale carved the turkey for the lunch, and their families and Dr Stephens and his family from Lechlade would all come and join the patients for tea. It made Christmas like

a big family occasion. I remember one elderly lady telling me that Dr Shaw had fetched in her buckets of coal when he visited her. There were numerous tales of how kind and caring they were.

It is one of the greatest values of being a small community hospital because you are dealing with local people. We still had the old operating theatre, although no operations took place after Dr Bloxsome's time – now that has been incorporated into the Day Hospital section. There was no children's ward, but we did have some children admitted, babies and toddlers would be put into cots in the women's ward. At that time, too, we still had our own hospital garden, so the patients all had fresh-grown vegetables. Our gardener was always in black with a black beret – we affectionately called him Hellfire Jack. The garden was later requisitioned by the County to extend the primary school playing field, then when the school was moved the land was sold and The Orchard, a new housing development, was built on it.

Ruth Batty

Patients And Preservation

I took over the Fairford medical practice half a century ago and lodged at Croft House for a while, Mrs Bloxsome drove Dr Harold and me around to introduce me to his patients as he was by then too ill to carry on. The speaking tube which his father had installed for night-time calls was still on the right-hand side of the side door, but was superseded by the telephone in my time. The small waiting room was on the left of the side door and the even smaller surgery was on the right, mainly occupied with bottles. Patients had to go down the long passage to the library to be examined.

I then lodged at Keble House, which had been the surgery in the time of the Drs Cornwall. There was certainly a presence about the old house. I remember one night one of the bells on the servants call board rang quite alarmingly as no one was around at the time, and old Nellie Luker, who had worked for the indomitable Misses Keble, would not go upstairs alone to start the domestic duties 'for fear of meeting Miss Mary'. I ran the practice single-handed at Croft House for about a year – as had my predecessors for most of their time, but in their respective days one called the doctor almost

as a last resort. In pre-National Health Service times there was markedly more concern for the health of the family pig – an ailing porker boded ill for the winter store of salted ham, so it was disastrous if the pig died before it was killed. The majority of families had their own cure-alls by which to keep them and anyone else going. In the early fifties the NHS urged everyone to 'consult their doctor' more on principle than judgment and I was lucky to get a day off a month. The 'day off' was in reality what was left of it after morning surgery – often it was already eleven o'clock before I could get on my bike and hurry down to the station. You could leave your bike in Mr Willis's garden at the Railway Cottages for one penny. He had a little dog I remember, he was grey-haired and had a nice smiley face – Mr Willis, I mean, not the dog! The midday Fairford Flyer took me to Oxford where I would have lunch at The Mitre, then go to Salters Yard and hire a skiff and spend the afternoon rowing up and down the Isis before returning home. On the even rarer occasions when I finished an hour earlier I would cycle to Oxford, then put the bicycle on the train to come back. As soon as I was back I was on call again.

After a year or so, I got Michael Veale in as assistant doctor. He was absolutely wonderful; after six months I made him a partner in the practice and we bought Hilary Cottage, which had been the old Ebenezer chapel, as the new surgery and we shared the cottage next door until we both married and lived off the premises – thus breaking the tradition of the doctoring families of Cornwall and Bloxsome. The old people used to tell of the Ebenezer chapel folk's graves being 'under the big mound in the Hilary Cottage garden' but we never experienced any ghostly goings-on. However, when Betty and I moved to the Croft and bought the old

Dr Charlton Shaw, the bridegroom (left) and Dr Michael Veale, his best man.

Congregational chapel and ground we did have the minister come to exorcise the site before the memorial stones were removed to the Baptist chapel. We retained what we call the 'little house' which is probably the oldest part of the chapel and reinstated the original foundation stone which we found during the making of our garden.

Some of the characters I've dealt with could have stepped out of Arthur Gibbs's chronicle of country life at the end of the Victorian era. There is my oft-quoted tale of the son of one old couple coming to the surgery to query the dosage of the medicine prescribed to his father. That was at the time when it was still normal to prescribe a wineglass measure. 'Mother says you got down 'ere that our Dad 'as to take a 'alf-a-wine-glass of that medicine – well, 'er wants to know which 'alf of the glass he got to drink.'

I remember being summoned out to one of my village patients and found him in a small room filled with black smoke. I could only just make him out amongst the pile of old horse blankets on the floor, his lizardy little face was just peeping over the top smoking the most foul-smelling pipe. 'Ah, Doctor,' he spluttered, 'I wants you to give I some of that pink tack as you gives I for me cough.' I told him I had to examine him first. He reluctantly fumbled about under the blankets to reveal about one inch of his chest. I told him that was no good and after a great deal of argument I helped him to peel off several woolly jumpers, two thick Oxford shirts and several layers of vests so that I could carry out a proper examination. 'Oh, dear, Doctor,' he said, 'thee bist more bloody trouble to I than thee be worth.' I reckon I could never get a better compliment!

There must be something in the age-old feeling, particularly in a country area, about turning to the family doctor with all kinds of problems – which aren't necessarily medically related, and that is how the Fairford Preservation Society evolved. A number of people were coming to me anxious about rumours of building all kinds of new things in all kinds of places: there was concern that a main road was going to cut across a quiet corner of the town, that cottages in London Street were in danger of being demolished to make way for 'nice bungalows'; the government of the day was all for 'modernizing' old places. When the concerns became specific, such as Nan Elliot being told that her dear little Wood Cottage, of which she was so rightly proud, was 'unfit for human habitation' simply on account of the ceiling being exactly half an inch too low to meet the new regulations, and the ancient row of cottages in East End was scheduled for demolition in favour of a new development, I explored the possibility of getting a preservation society such as was springing up in other parts of the country where the heritage of a place was under threat. One old chap from East End came to me in great distress because a gentleman had been to see him to find out about him drinking water from the well in his garden – which his family had done for generations to no ill effect. However, the gentleman returned and had a workman fill the well with rubble to stop 'this unhealthy habit'. This meant that the old chap simply went along to his sister, who lived in the same row of cottages, and drew his drinking water from her well and lived a long and healthy life ever after!

I think I must have written well over a hundred letters to such 'gentlemen' along with MPs and anyone else whom I thought might be interested. I would have written to the Queen – if I could spell Queen! Anyway, the cottages were reprieved and the Society has been instrumental in fighting for the preservation of what we all love about Fairford and is still going strong after some forty-odd years.

Charlton Shaw

Partners In Practice

It was Dr Jim Grove-White that I have to thank for introducing me to Charlton Shaw; he said that there was a young doc-

Dr Charlton and Mrs Betty Shaw with Dr Michael and Mrs Angela Veale at centre table of RNA dinner. Mrs John Busby (left), Mr and Mrs Archie Spalding in front.

Nancy Thornton ('driving') and her sister, Doddie, on their tandem tricycle, 1965.

tor fresh out of the Navy running the Fairford Practice on his own and he thought we ought to meet, we would have a lot in common. We did. That was in 1951. It was an exceedingly happy partnership and looking back I realize how much more we were left pretty much to our own devices on how we run the practice – just the two of us, with Nan Elliott to keep us in order and holding the fort when we were not in surgery. Nan lived in the flat at Hilary Cottage and when Charlton and I went hunting with the VWH on a Saturday Nan had the use of our Morris Minor, which was the official practice car, to trundle out into the countryside to fetch us if there was an emergency.

We take pride that it was Charlton and me who put Fairford Cottage Hospital on the present footing. When we first came the then Matron obviously didn't take kindly to these young bachelor doctors: Shaw and Veale could do nothing right for her; she adored Dr Morgan from Lechlade, and it became obvious that there was a bias towards whose patients were being admitted. The final straw broke when she snorted 'I'm not taking that sort of person in here – that patient is verminous!' It was as though I had purposely sought out someone who was literally crawling just to annoy her, when my chief concern was that it was a patient in need of hospital treatment.

Charlton and I wreaked our revenge by building a huge snowman in front of the hospital's front door under cover of darkness – we were careful to keep the outpatients' emergency doorway clear –

and pelted her bedroom window which was just above the front porch with snowballs. We had made a fair escape by the time she had come down the stairs to be confronted by our snowman at the door, then negotiated the warren of passages to get out to hurl abuse at the culprits – whom she never found!

Eventually after a catalogue of events, the hospital was closed completely. It re-opened under a completely new structure with Ruth Batty as Sister-in-charge, its own governing body, and retained its autonomy under the administration of Cirencester and its Matron. A grateful patient donated £20 for whatever purpose Sister Batty chose, and she gave it to me to start the Physiotherapy Fund which I had been anxious to augment. That was in 1971 and has grown ever since, thanks to the help and support of so many local people. In the early days we all collected newspapers and when we had a truckload Richard Freeth gave the Fund so much a ton: Tom Boulton and Nancy Thornton, particularly, worked tirelessly, collecting and sorting and tying them up in bundles; Nancy even went articulated in the cause – towing a home-made trailer on the back of her three-wheeler tricycle to collect the papers.

Now, thirty years later, the Physiotherapy Fund has just amalgamated with the League of Friends of Fairford Hospital, so that the patients of both Fairford and Lechlade practices can benefit from a range of services and improvements provided from the fund-raising efforts and voluntary support of so many people.

What a happy half a century – how very kind the community has been.

Michael Veale

Half A Century At The Clinic

The first baby clinic of what became known as Lechlade and District Child Welfare Centre was opened just before Christmas in 1950. Mrs Richardson of Southrop Manor officially opened it in the Memorial Hall. I remember, before that, when my daughter, Maureen, was a baby we went to Nurse Twinning's cottage, next door to the Hall to get the babies weighed and collect orange juice. Nurse Keeling was the next District Nurse and she really got the idea of a clinic going. We formed a committee to run it and the Health Authority provided some equipment, but there was also quite a lot lent by local people. We had white screens set up in the Hall and there were playpens for the children and lots of toys to play with, all the orange juice and tinned milk and cod liver oil were set out on trestle tables and it all looked very professional. The ladies' dressing room was turned into the doctor's surgery for the duration of the clinic – the clinic doctor at that time wasn't local. We had a lot of keen helpers and Mrs Rushby kept us all supplied with tea and hot water.

I was invited to join the committee – Nurse Day of Eastleach was our president, the clinic covered Eastleach and Southrop as well as Lechlade. Miss Bluett helped with several other ladies with the clerical work and Margaret Hatton was appointed treasurer, she was treasurer for over forty years. I had always been interested in young children and had been a teacher before I got married. In those days the Education Authority wouldn't employ married teachers, so I was very happy to do the voluntary work at the clinic – weighing the babies and keeping an eye on the children generally, distributing the baby food and keeping the register.

Mrs Margaret Hatton, Mrs Winifred Smith and Mrs Stacey, founder members of the Lechlade Clinic, c. 1960.

Nurse Davis at Fairford Clinic during the 1930s.

The clinic was held once a month to start with, then it became once a fortnight and eventually each week as the area widened. We always had a hard-working committee and we held fund-raising events, mainly rummage sales, for the Christmas parties so that every child had a present. We also had a summer party – these used to be held at either Mrs Richardson's at Southrop, or Mrs Honour's at Eastleach. Mostly we bought the toys locally – from the Black Cat, or Mr Lee's or Mr Powell's, they were all well stocked shops. The clinic catered for children from birth to starting school age, but mostly we didn't see much of them after they were about three years old, except for their preschool vaccinations. When the new medical centre was built, just inside the old Manor grounds, the clinic moved there with, of course, our own practice doctors.

Over the years we have had a great number of helpers – but Mrs Hatton and I have just completed fifty years together since the clinic first started, and as we are both in our late eighties we felt it was time to retire. I suppose the greatest noticeable change has been in babies' dress – they used to be in binders and back flannels, nappies were towelling – disposables hadn't been heard of then – and long gowns and bonnets. But children themselves don't really change, no matter how fashions do.

Winifred Smith

A Family Of Family Doctors

I come from a family of doctors, and my wife and our children are all doctors. When I took over the Lechlade practice from Dr Morgan

Drs David, Henry and Sheila Stephens.

in 1956 I ran it virtually single-handed; there was no practice nurse, no secretary, not even a typewriter. I spent a large part of every evening writing letters and dealing with the paperwork by hand. The district nurse had to cope with the community and nursing and welfare and home confinements were still the normal practice. For the first year I rented two rooms in Dr Morgan's house, then I had the wooden prefab built in my own garden and it served us well for over twenty-five years. Eventually it became possible to buy a corner of land from the Convent and our new medical centre, which houses the surgery and clinic, opened in 1981 and was enlarged in 1996.

My wife, Sheila, joined the practice as my partner after the first ten years, so we are always referred to as Dr David or Dr Sheila; now that our son has taken over from us, he is known as Dr Henry. This is a very close-knit, supportive community and in the early days there was a great deal of home visiting, so one got to know the patients extremely well. In some of the neighbouring villages there was still no indoor sanitation – it was very much a matter of a bucket at the top of the garden in an old privy. I remember visiting one patient in a particularly bad winter, only to find the water in a glass by his bedside was frozen absolutely solid. There was certainly no such thing as central heating in the majority of cottages.

Lechlade and Fairford are two very different places, but are bound together by the Cottage Hospital and other branches on the medical front, and socially through our musical activities – but there is great sporting rivalry still. Now inter-county reservation is a different matter altogether, and must date back to the old moonraker tales days. Lechlade is the meeting point of what used to be four counties, and I used to have four different prescription pads for the appropriate county authority to cover patients who were served by the practice, but lived 'over the border'. I have known on more than one occasion of a drowning in the Thames when the body was recovered the boat was pushed across to the other side of the river.

David Stephens

CHAPTER 5
Church, Chapel and Convent

Fairford Church.

Robert Kimber (from a pen and ink drawing), c. 1840.

The Poor Man's Bible

That was the popular name for the medieval set of twenty-eight stained glass windows in St Mary's church. The most graphic account of the scriptural scenes was, surely, that as given by Robert Kimber, the Victorian parish clerk, whose homely rendering in his native Gloucestershire tongue was captured verbatim in 1866:

The upper part o' that winda you zee (pausing before the great West Window) is a representation of the daay o' judgment. In the centre is Christ. E's a zittin on the rainbow. Ther's the earth for 'is footstool. E's surrounded you zee by cherabins and zeraphins all a zitting round the blue circle looking up to 'im. Now, at the bottom ther, that's wer ther going to judgment with ther graveclothes on, jest a comin up. Farther on you zee is a large figure ther most of it yalla. That's Saynt Michul. E's a wayin a good person in one scale against a bad un in another. Wer the good un ought to ha' bin ther's a bit o' common glass. In that yalla scale close at 'is right ther's a little red devul sittin ther wi' yalla hyes a hendeavouring to turn the scale, but the good outways the bad. In the next cumpartment is a hangel ther with yalla 'air. Now we cums to the representation of 'ell. In the corner ther is owld Belzebub with red and white tith (teeth). E's got a scaly face and a big fish's mouth. And jest above 'is ed to the right ther's small figures a sprawling ther arms out wer ther put in tarment – and ther's wer ther a rackin and a grindin on em. Close against the weel ther's a little red devul with a crown on 'is ed and yalla hyes to turn the andle for'n. This eere is a curious hidea – but it's accardin to awld istory. This is a warnin to all females (tapping the figure on the glass with the long fishing rod, its tip covered with a scrap of chamois leather – which he used as a pointer) – that's a devul a weeling a ooman off to 'ell in a weelbarra for scowldin on 'er 'usband. She looks to be a scowld, zir, a gwain off back'ards, zir. Ther's the weel of the barra painted yalla and ther's th' andle, an the blue devul delighted anough a bowlin of 'er off ther. I had a party o' gen'lemen and ladies ere th' other week; ther was a owld gent who didn't agree with it all; 'e sed 'e felt for she altogether as was gwain in the cart, she looked so good-tempered; but as for th' other, 'e and't no pity for 'er. E set the ladies a laffin, 'e did, an thay didn't stop durin the time thay was in the church.

Robert Kimber

Frightened Into Faith?

To welcome the great West Window back to St Mary's, after its restoration by Keith Barley, our conservator, in December 2000 posed me something of a problem, because, as the old parish clerk was reported as describing the scene, it illustrates Christ as sitting in judgement, assisted by St Michael with a pair of scales. On the left are the golden courts of the Kingdom of Heaven. On the right is a much more colourful and vivacious picture: devils carting off souls towards Lucifer, whose wide mouth devours the terrified figures of the damned. I wondered anew about the message it set out to convey in its restored glowing colours and art form, and I was aware of how much late medieval theology set out to so graphically persuade worshippers to seek the Kingdom of Heaven through fear of the pains of Hell.

The point I made in the sermon I preached to welcome back the window was as a reminder that it should be the love and forgiveness of the Saviour which draws us into obedience to His Word – and not fear! But do the Fairford devils have any place in our thinking about God? Is God so understanding that we shall all find a place in Heaven, even if we have not made much effort to follow Our Lord here on earth? The answer may lie in part in the story of 'Chopsticks' – one of my favourites. It is a legend about a native warrior who died and went to Heaven, but before he entered the gate he requested a guided tour of Hell. To his amazement a great table was piled with wonderful food, as it was in Heaven, the only difference he could see between the two places was in the people; in Hell they were starving, in Heaven they were happy and well-fed – yet both places only provided 5ft-long chopsticks, which no one could manage to eat with. The answer lies in the fact that in Heaven everyone had learned that if a man fed his neighbour, his neighbour will feed him also.

John Willard

Named But Not Christened

One day we were sent to play all day long in our toy-shed. We didn't know why until 'I was old enough' to be told. Apparently my Mum gave birth at seven months to a daughter, who was hastily named as Clare by the midwife, but the baby died. The vicar, the Revd Sale, came to our house but would not have a proper funeral for Clare as she was not baptized. My dad was so upset because she had to be buried round the back of the church in unconsecrated ground because, the Revd Sale said, if she was not baptized she was classed as a sinner. My dad swore he would never go to church again, but he did – for my sake, to come to see me married to Dick – his name was also Cooper, so I was a Miss Cooper who became Mrs Cooper.

Gramp Cooper is buried in St Lawrence's churchyard, down by the school gates, and sometimes I would wander on round to the back of the church to where my little sister, who didn't live long enough for any of us to know, was laid to rest. I couldn't understand it – the spot was always just as green and grassy as the whole of the registered churchyard.

Peggy Cooper

Convent Days

I started at St Clotilde's as a day girl, but soon realized that all the fun took place after school hours so I pleaded with my parents to let me be a boarder. I loved it and my poor unsuspecting parents let me stay on. It wasn't until we were in the sixth form that we realized how naïve we had been in the earlier years when we thought we were so clever at breaking school rules. Sister Mary St Edmund, known affectionately among us as Eddie, really treated us as adults then. 'Do you really think that we didn't know you smoked in the Green Bathroom – you just can't disguise the smell of cigarettes no matter how much talc you throw over you, or splash on the deodorant, besides which throwing the butt ends out of the window wasn't too clever – I simply walked round, stood under the window and collected the evidence!' She probably sussed out that our carefully guarded code name of our meeting place, was devised from the favoured smokes of the day. Our password was 'We'll meet at Peter Benson's'; that was near the hockey field in a secret spot just behind the small cemetery.

I remember Eddie catching me once climbing out of the window, which we often did to save the long walk through the old Manor to the door. She asked if that was the way my family and I made our exit from our home in Southrop. It really put me in my place and made me respect the fact that though the Convent was a school it was our home for the time we were there. We always seemed to be up to some kind of prank – one midnight feast in the attic, which could only be reached through a trap door and precariously straddling the four-by-four timbers as there was no proper flooring, ended in bringing down both the wrath of the nuns and the dormitory ceiling when Emma Holt forgot about the straddle technique and stepped down on to the flimsy flooring. She was stuck there with her leg waving around through

Convent girls in classroom, 1971. From left to right, standing: Deborah Martyr, Patricia Calnan, Emma Holt. Sitting: Sarah Iles, Sally Chesterton, Celia Minoprio.

the dormitory ceiling – that was more than enough evidence of what was going on.

The poor nuns, I do believe we led them a merry dance. They did seem to spend an awful lot of time chasing the village boys away from the old stable block where the new dormitories were. We were allowed to go into Lechlade as long as we wore our hat. This was a sort of papal cap with the school badge in front. The uniform was a grey skirt, with lilac blouse and white-striped purple tie, and long grey socks with a mauve top band. The blouses were later white. It was the age of the miniskirt and we had to kneel in line in front of Eddie – nothing to do with communal prayer – it was to enable her to measure our skirt length, which was strictly limited to no more than 4in higher than our knees when we were in a kneeling position.

We spent hours on end loitering on one of the road junctions counting the number of passing vehicles – this was under the auspicious title of environmental research and was supposed to be of value in the fight to get a by-pass. Our strongest field was in the Arts – English, Languages, particularly with Drama and trying to turn us into cultured young ladies. However, I always ended up as being cast as the local yokel or drunken lout in the school productions, although I was assured by our Music and Drama teacher, that it was only because I had a good, strong voice which carried well to the back of the gym, where we staged our performances!

I certainly enjoyed my time at the Convent, I am conscious that there is and always seems to have been a certain aura attached to the term 'Convent girl', but equally aware that there is a sort of 'naughty girls' reputation as well, and was rather boastful of the fact that Bridget Bardot went to St Clotilde – but that was in France, of course!

Sarah More

From Student To Teacher

I do remember Sarah, in fact when this bright young girl stood up in my class to recite a poem by Walter de la Mare I looked across at her thinking that she was play-acting the part – the recitation was rendered in such a perfect local voice, and it reminded me of how my elocution lessons had started. I had been teaching Music and Drama to girls from all over the country, many of which had such pronounced regional accents that it was quite difficult for them to be understood. It was at the time that there was a very distinct 'BBC speech' and this did have an influence on a move towards speaking 'Standard English' which would be understood throughout the country in the different professions.

I was a pupil at St Clotilde's for three years during the war – absolute bliss to be in a quiet country manor house after spending so many nights in a damp and cold air-raid shelter. The Convent had only just started in Lechlade in 1939. The move was also for it to have a country background. The school then was very small: about three in a class, it was like having one's own governesses. Sister Mary St Edmund was there from the beginning – a very young nun, only thirteen years

Convent of St Clotilde, June 1971.

older than I was at the time. She was such fun, but appeared to be quite delicate. When she took us for Games lessons she would pin up the top layer of the many skirts of her habit so that she could run easier. She epitomized the true English lady of English-Irish ancestry.

St Clotilde's was a French Order. The concept of the Convent originally stemmed from a kindly lady who took pity on the orphans from the French Revolution; the orphanage later became a Convent. From the outset it was founded for the children of the wealthier families – unlike other convents at the time which were for the poorest of the poor. Later the founding ladies took their vows and gained papal recognition as an Order. The habit of the nuns of St Clotilde's was exactly the same as the foundresses wore: full-length black gowns with black bonnets, edged with hand-goffered, starched white frills. It was the habit which separated them from the rest of the community. Later, in an attempt to modernize their image, it was stream-lined – designed by Dior – slimmer, smart dresses with mid-length skirts; he did away with the bonnets but the heads were still covered; they were still recognizably nuns. The final stage was the transition into jumpers and skirts with the idea that they should no longer be separated from the rest of humanity – I consider this an absolute pity. The distinctive habit was symbolic of their dedication to their calling and one felt that a nun could be approached for some kind of help or comfort in time of trouble.

There were a number of other convents of St Clotilde's, but the Order is now dying out and the nuns from Lechlade have now been returned to the Mother House in Reuilly, near Paris, when the old Manor was sold in 1998. The Convent chapel has been de-consecrated and many Catholics now worship at St Thomas's church at Horcott, although the Methodist chapel in Lechlade very generously offer their building for the celebration of Mass each week. The closure of the Convent has ended yet another chapter in local history; some of the furnishings are in use at St Thomas's and the Statue of Our Lady has been erected in the grounds of the Presbytery. The statue of Christ the King, in the churchyard, came from the Fairford Polish Camp chapel. It had been presented to the Polish community by the Americans when they first came to the RAF base at Fairford. What a mix of international involvement is illustrated in and around the Church!

June Howell

Changes

I wasn't forced to change my religion when I married Tino, but of course Italians are very devout Catholics and I thought about it for a long time before I became a convert. I am quite happy now, at first it was strange because there are more regulations and confessions which I wasn't used to. But now, there are concessions made. The old confessional box has been replaced by a curtain, and you have the choice of going behind it, or facing the priest – also, if you don't want to make your confession to your own parish priest, you can opt to be heard by a visiting priest. I think, in a way, it is a good thing to have to stop and think about what you have done or said. We only have Latin for special occasions, and then most of us women wear a black lace veil to cover our head. Not so long ago, women were not allowed into

Roman Catholic church of St Thomas and Presbytery, Horcott.

a Catholic church with bared arms or head. I think it is nice if people do pay respect to the church occasion.

Peggy Corso

Followers From Afar

I have been a member of St Thomas of Canterbury Roman Catholic church at Horcott since 1942, when I came to Fairford as an Italian prisoner of war to work for Mr Ken Iles at Park Farm. Four of us lived in Number 14 Park Street, and Italians from farms at Eastleach and Meysey Hampton used to cycle in to church. Father McSweeney was the priest then, he was well-loved and well-respected by everyone, and one of the windows – St Patrick's, was given to the church by the Irish workers who built the RAF base as a thank you to Father. Later on, when the Americans took over the base, they loved him so much that they collected enough money to send him to America for a holiday.

Peggy and I got married at St Thomas's, then we went back to my home in Italy for a few years, but returned here to bring up our family. Father Roche was another good priest. He came in 1962 and did such a lot to restore the church and the Presbytery. He started the Friday night bingo to raise the money. That was a big thing for Fairford – Friday night Bingo – the Palmer Hall used to be packed for it. He used to go down to Bristol every month to get the prizes – good prizes they were, too. He put in proper heating, there were only paraffin heaters before, and a lovely wood block floor and all sorts of improvements.

Polish free-fighters at the Park Camp, c. 1950. Edward Czopek (far left of front line) made Fairford his home.

There are several reminders of the Polish camp that was up in the Park after the war, and the churchyard is more than half filled with Polish graves. Every year on All Souls' and All Saints' Days their relatives come and leave lighted candles, in decorated holders – just like we have in Italy – to burn all night on the graves.

Tino Corso

Chapels As United Church

I studied the life and work of the Nonconformist churches in Fairford for my A-level project in 1970 and I was surprised to find that Nonconformity had, in fact, started as early as the reign of Elizabeth I when a site in the Croft was granted for the Congregational chapel. It was founded in

1662 – the year that the Ejectment Order was published. This foundation was most probably for a licensed house, referred to as 'the old Meeting House' which was replaced in 1744 by a purpose-built chapel, it was enlarged in 1817, but again was replaced by the last chapel to be built on the site in 1862, financed by H.O. Wills of Bristol, a founder of the tobacco firm. The old transept was incorporated in the Gothic style of the chapel, which was built for an estimated cost of £900.

In the early days the break away from the established Church caused quite a division in the community. There is an interesting story, similar to two of the plagues of Egypt, which stems from that time: on 24 June 1660 a company of Nonconformists, probably Baptists, were on their way to a private meeting when they were abused by some of the Fairford townsfolk. The Lord of the Manor,

Congregational chapel in the Croft, being dismantled, 1966.

Fairford Chapel Sunday school Christmas party, 1954. Beryl Law at back, holding her daughter, Miriam.

An historic moment for Sarah Bennett, looking at the baptistry uncovered for the first time in half a century ready for her baptism by total immersion in 1988 at Fairford.

standing by. Retribution followed swiftly by a plague of Caddis flies, with long wings, settling in the manorial orchard wrecking the crop. Several inhabitants of the town swore to the truth of this tale and enquirers from London noted that the windows of the Dissenters' meeting house were broken.

Other chapels were built at the west end of the town: the Ebenezer chapel was erected in 1744 but closed during the early 1900s and later became the doctors' surgery under the name of Hilary Cottage; and the Primitive Methodist chapel built in 1867 was in Wicks' Yard in Coronation Street. That, too, closed and became the headquarters for the Scouts until it was sold to become a private house.

The only chapel to remain today is the old Baptist chapel in Milton Street, built in 1853, replacing a meeting house of 1723. When all the old Baptists died out it became the Congregational in 1951, but records show that there was a union in 1919, with united worship held alternatively in the Baptist and Congregational chapels in 1883. Now it is officially known as Fairford United church and the unity with both the Anglican and Roman Catholic communities has strengthened over the most recent years.

Miriam Law

It Was An Ill Wind....

We came to Fairford House in 1969 and within a few months Edward Keble had invited me to join the PCC. There was an urgent need to re-lead the church roof and to renew the wire guards in an attempt to preserve the stained glass windows against further damage, but there was just no money available. Then came the mini-hurricane in 1971.

who practically ruled the town, looked on and did nothing to stop the unprovoked attack. That evening many thousands of toads came up Mill Lane, they divided into two companies. One went to the Manor House and could not be prevented from entering. They swarmed into the kitchen and into the cellar. The house was relieved the next morning by an 'honest member of the household'. The second division of the toads went into the barn of the Justice of the Peace, who said it was a judgement following the abuse of the Nonconformists. About a fortnight later, the same kind of incident occurred, again with the Lord of the Manor

Unusually, Betty and I were not in church that Sunday morning. We were looking out of the window across the river and suddenly saw branches literally blowing off the old Wellingtonia trees and hurled across the grass. A great thump on the window, a tearing rush of roaring wind and then it was all over in a minute. I put on my gumboots to see whatever was going on. The drive was completely blocked by the top of one of the beech trees. I looked up at the church: twin pinnacles from one corner of the tower had been ripped off – fortunately, because the wind had come up from the south-west, they had fallen into the middle of the tower – had they gone through the roof it would have been an absolute tragedy as Matins had not yet finished. The parapet was completely stripped of its line of single pinnacles – they lay shattered all over the churchyard.

The devastation to our lovely old church was on everyone's lips, of course, and the freak storm or mini-hurricane or whatever it was called attracted a great deal of attention in the press. But, in a strange sort of way – it's an ill wind, as they say, because here was the objective to do fund-raising on a big scale. Re-roofing and replacing window guards are not the sort of projects, necessary as they are, to whip up enthusiastic generosity – but the pinnacles were wonderful. Everyone could see them, and the church without them was just too awful – so it was timely to stage a festival, which we had previously thought about. Now, it would be special – the first of its kind in Fairford. Flower festivals were just making their appearance and St Mary's was the ideal stage for it, and, of course, the object of the event.

I was made chairman of the festival committee and I set out about organizing it as a naval command officer would: everyone on the committee had a specific job, which they carried out in a most excellent manner. I was proud to have taken them on board! The church was just full of flowers with displays of vestments and deanery silver – that was wonderful, to have such an important collection from the parishes – much of it dating back to Elizabethan times and, of immense interest – the Fairford Mazer, as old as the church itself. We had to make sure that it was guarded day and night. Flower ladies are quite powerful people – I know I had to treat the Flower Queen Bee, as I called her, with almost the same deference as one reserves for royalty when she came to view the ladies' efforts.

We had other wonderful exhibitions as well: personal possessions of John Keble were displayed in Keble House, his birthplace, so that was very appropriate. The ladies of the WI arranged an arts and crafts exhibition in the Palmer Hall and Mrs Joss Barker very kindly had some very valuable and most interesting deeds and documents from the County archives on display in her house. Gardens in the Croft, the smaller ones as well as the really wonderful garden that Miss Dugdale and Miss Scott created at Croft House – our own garden was open, of course, as well. Fairford Silver Band did us proud over the weekend, as they always have, and there were stalls lining the High Street under the church wall.

Heather Ansell, the festival secretary, and Bertie Champion did such a good job of the publicity that Park Street was lined with coaches and there were long queues to get into the church. There was also a great fun donkey derby on the Saturday, with picnics in the Park. It really was a mammoth event, and so many people worked so hard to make it the huge success it was. It really was incredible that little Fairford could raise that sort of money – £5,500 in one weekend. Me?

Peter Juggins with one of the pinnacles he carved to replace the fifteenth-century ones destroyed in the freak whirlwind of 1971.

Well, I must admit that because everyone pulled their weight everything went like clockwork – and Melba Barnfield had kindly let me have her drawing room in Montague House as my 'command post' as it was so strategically placed opposite the church – so I went there 'on duty' in the afternoon and enjoyed a really quiet gin and tonic!

Laurie Carey

Bells And Ringers

I grew up with the sound of St Lawrence's church bells chiming through my bedroom window. My mother used to hold a Sunday school in our cottage so I was attached to the church from a very early age. Alf King taught me to ring the bells. He used to tell me that the five oldest bells of the six were quarter-tuned and hung with a new treble in '19 ought 11'. Alf was a great churchman – he was Tower Captain for years and a keen chorister and had a wonderful ear for music. I remember once when we dashed round to the vestry to get robed up we met Dr Stephens who was our choirmaster at the time and he asked Alf how his ear was – 'Ah,' said Alf, 'you know, Doctor, since you syringed it for me it's that good I could hear a mouse doing the twist'. Even after he suffered a stroke and his speech was impaired, Alf still retained his musical sense and insisted on still being in the choir. He could not articulate the words, but he accompanied us all with his perfectly pitched 'lahs' throughout. What a great character he was and I was proud to follow him as Tower Captain nearly forty years ago.

One instance of our bell-ringing team's dedication was on New Year's Day 1962. We had been ringing out the Old Year and ringing in the New at midnight and left the bells up ready to ring the next morning – well, it was only going to be in a few hours' time. During the night there was the memorable snowstorm. We duly fought our way to the church and started to ring for the service, and we were absolutely showered with snow from where it had blown in through the tower louvers and caught in the bells. We were trying to make the best of being thoroughly drenched and bitterly cold when Mr Fawkes came to tell us that there would be no service after all – we were between vicars and the stand-in vicar was snowed in.

Ray Hayden

Thereby Hangs A Tale

'Some will have observed that the church weathercock had been absent from his perch for some seven or eight months. The malady from which he suffered was one of an internal nature and necessitated very invasive surgery, i.e. splitting him completely down the middle, rebushing and relocating his 'innards', skeletal reinforcement, external skin-grafting, contusions remedied and a First or Second World War suspected 0.303 bullet wound in the posterior region required additional surgery.'
Bodgitt, late of Bodgitt and Scapa

Yes, it was me that wrote that little piece for our parish news explaining why the church weathercock was 'missing presumed …' recently. When the scaffolding was up for the work on the tower I was able to look at it more closely. It was in a parlous condition. The pivot was worn through the top of the body, so I undertook the job of repairing and re-gilding it. I can't understand how it got so badly dented. The body is in two halves, rather like a chocolate Easter egg is made, then they overlap by about half an inch and soft soldered. The body extends up into the neck of the head and the tail is riveted to the body. There must be a tale to tell of how the poor old bird got a bullet hole in its tail. What was exciting was to find the name of the maker on the portion of the tail which is sandwiched between the two body halves: 'Joseph Packer, Maker, Cirencester 1843.'

The cock weighs about 13lbs and is made from copper. I have double gilded it with twenty-three-and-a-half carat double thickness English gold leaf – the English gold leaf being the most superior of its continental rivals for this job. The gold is in transfer leaf form and so fine that I couldn't measure it

on my micrometer – it is less than one-tenth of one-thousandth of an inch. Thank goodness it's not powder, I would be frightened to sneeze. It is applied to a special size, which can be used in various time scales, so it is important to time the processes very carefully, because the solvent in the size has to dry to just the right consistency for the gold to adhere successfully. I calculate this stage by the size just dragging on the back of my finger and making the slightest squeak. Gold is very dense so it is crucial not to put it on until the solvent has had time to evaporate, but not to leave it too long otherwise it will not stick. Yes, of course, gold leaf is the most expensive finish and you might wonder why it is used on something like the weathercock which is so far up that its finer finish can't be appreciated, but gold is highly reflective and endurable. It will outlive paint by three or four times, and in its exposed position the old cock should still look respectable in

Derrick Youngs repairing St Mary's Church weathercock.

another quarter of a century.

It is rewarding to think that I can contribute to the continuity of the old-time craftsmen, so on the other side of the maker's name, which was stamped in the tail piece which is sandwiched between the two body halves, I've inscribed: 'Repaired by Derrick Youngs, Fairford 2000.'

If you look up at the cockerel on Cirencester parish church you will see that it is a perfect pair to ours at St Mary's – so probably made also by Joseph Packer – they must have hatched from the same clutch of church cock eggs!

Derrick Youngs

Tiddles, From Stray To Celebrity

I was verger at St Mary's when I first met Tiddles – a thin and weakly little tabby cat drinking out of the flower vases in the churchyard. It looked so pitiful and when it came back day after day, obviously a stray and uncared for, I went across to Radways the baker's and got it some food. Well, that was the start of our friendship. I took it something every day and let it into the church rooms to sleep. Eventually she got so attached to me that she followed me into the church and made it her home for the next seventeen years! I named her Tiddles. She was a wonderful mouser and became part of the congregation, favouring different laps or shoulders during the services. Canon Keble was a great animal lover so was quite happy for Tiddles to be one of the flock – and she wasn't above watching the service from the pulpit. She liked to see what was going on, she was a sort of watchdog-cat. When Vera, my wife, was doing her brass rubbings to raise money for the church, Tiddles would sit on John Tame's tomb to keep her company.

One day at a funeral service Tiddles settled under the pew below the window filled

Tiddles when she was church cat (1963-1980).

84

with terrible-looking devils, and came creeping out under the overcoat of one of the mourners. Well, poor fellow, it nearly frightened the life out of him. It must have felt like an unseen hand touching his leg. She made her presence felt again during the flower festival of 1972. The deanery silver was on display in the church, as you can imagine we had to make sure we had good security, so two of the churchwardens stopped in the church all night as well as having a special system installed. Suddenly the alarm went off in the middle of the night and the police arrived. There was no sign of any intruder, then all of a sudden there was this little 'Meow', and there was the culprit – our Tiddles had strayed across the security beam and set off the alarm. We were all very upset when she died, but I wanted her to be returned to the home she had adopted, and Canon Keble agreed to my request to have her buried in the churchyard. In fact, he conducted a little service for her and there were quite a few mourners to see her laid to rest – in the most prominent spot in the churchyard, too, facing the front entrance along with the notables of the town. I had the little memorial carved by Peter Juggins, a wonderful stone mason who did all the pinnacles on the church and replaced a lot of the figures after that terrible storm damage.

I think Tiddles must have the most photographed tomb in the country – it has been on television several times. Of course, after twenty years the nice creamy white stone has got a bit mottled with lichen, but I give old Tiddles a bit of a brush up when I can, and I think that patchy marking makes her look more like the colour she was in reality when she was the church cat.

Sidney Jacques

Sid Jacques holding a tapestry kneeler, in memory of Tiddles, behind her tomb.

Fairford To Fairford

When the Bishop of Gloucester came to Fairford in June 1998 to celebrate the 500th anniversary of the consecration of the 'new' church of St Mary's he had some surprising company from Fairford: a party of twenty-six natives of the Ojibway tribe. June (our author) had established a link with the other Fairford when she visited the reservation in Manitoba, researching into the settlement founded by Abraham Cowley from this Fairford. The name of the North American Red Indian village was changed from Pinaymootang to the name of the missionary's birthplace as a tribute to his successful establishment of the Anglican church in the 1840s.

The Revd John Willard greets Lenny, an Ojibway Indian, and Father Ron McCullough from Fairford Reservation, Manitoba in 1998.

Headed by our Town Crier, the fully-feathered Fairfordians, two uniformed Canadian Mounties; Father Ron, their Anglican priest, and our own bishop and clergy splendidly attired, escorted by John and Peter, our churchwardens elegant in morning suits – what a spectacular procession we turned out as we walked from The Bull past the whirring television cameras and local onlookers to the west door of the church. The bishop hammered on the door to re-enact the events of 1497.

There was a point of reverential tradition to be resolved at that moment; something which could not have been dreamt of by John Tame's vicar – there were no fewer than three Red Indian chiefs, past, penultimate-past and present, all in flowing feathered headdress; how could we get through to them that men bared their head in church without offending their native pride? Our bishop diplomatically and graciously pointed out that as he was expected to wear his mitre in church then the Ojibway chiefs should wear their headdress – this was an important ceremonial occasion.

How proud our local man, Abraham Cowley, would have been to have seen his christianized Fairfordians in his home Fairford church. And what a moment that was when, a year later, one of the young Ojibway Indians read one of the lessons in his native tongue at the wedding of June and Ralph.

John Willard

CHAPTER 6
Trades, Farms and Shops

Margaret Whiteman looking at the doll's pram of her sister, Frances, with their brother, George.

Lamb In A Pram

As a small child I wasn't a bit interested in dolls, but when I inherited a doll's pram from my sister, Frances, I thought it was marvellous and put my pet lamb in it – the lamb obviously thought it was pretty good too, and would cuddle down in the pram while I pushed it from home at Cote Mill up Cellars Hill. We were told that the hill got its name because there were cellars under it, but we never found out whether that was true. My dad farmed all his life and did a fair amount of dealing in livestock so was a well-known figure at the local markets. He bought the sheep and cattle for Butcher Clack who turned it into lamb and beef at his shop behind Cobblestones in Eastleach. I remember the shop as being very large with grey slabs all round it, and there was a pound on the opposite side of the road where the animals were kept awaiting slaughter – it couldn't have been more local.

Mr and Mrs Whiteman at Cote Mill.

We kept Oxford Downs on the fields behind the old school at Eastleach and I spent all the time I could with old Shep Hunt and it was from him I developed my love for sheep. We kept the cattle at Lechlade in fields by the river at Downington and Frances, George and I loved to go with Dad to walk them to the market down by the railway station, and on occasion had to get them back home. Imagine driving a herd of cows along the main road through Lechlade today! It was quite an event and people used to shut their garden gate when they saw us coming and often walked alongside us to help keep them from straying. Once, when we were passing Jenkins the baker's, one of the cows saw its reflection in the shop window and thinking it was another cow tried to join it.

We loved our country life. There was always something of interest around us – fishing for sticklebacks in the River Leach at the bottom of our garden, rambling across the fields to Cote Farm, we always ran past Miss Philpott's cottage from the footpath, because she dressed from head to toe in long black clothes we imagined she must be a witch. In the wintertime we used to slide down the hill on a large tin tray to see who would get closest to the river, and in the springtime we each had our own pet lamb or calf to look after.

Mrs Frank Cox was our teacher at Southrop school, she would sit on the fireguard in front of the open fire and we would be mesmerized by the fact that she stuffed her hanky in her bloomer legs – if we leant back in our seat we could see what colour she wore. She was such a nice lady, more of a friend than a teacher, and we would stop and help her collect the eggs and, in the autumn pick up the fallen apples in her cottage garden next to the school. When it was our school sports day we collected sacks from the mill for the sack race, bounding and jumping along with Hinton's blazoned across the front. Some of them still had scraps of barley in them and if you didn't give them a good shake out first you had the prickly bits sticking in your knickers!

Our friends loved coming to our house at Cote Mill for tea because we had butter as well as jam on our bread – not only did our mum make all the juicy jam but the delicious golden butter as well. The milk was from our own cows and Mum skimmed off the cream, so we had luscious fresh cream with jam in the sponge cakes. We had a cosy family life. Even at an early age I felt privileged to live in the countryside to watch kingfishers in our lilac tree and be involved with the natural world around us. I thought we were ever so well off because we had two cars – really for Mum and Dad to do the school runs – and we had a telephone, but no electricity, so we never had television but we amused ourselves by playing cards, knitting and sewing and reading round the table under the light of the old oil lamps. All the cooking was done on a black-leaded range and we had no central heating. The corn mill next door had their own generator which started up precisely at seven o'clock every morning – so that was our alarm clock. Dead on ten o'clock my mum made a huge jug of hot chocolate for the mill workers, it was too heavy for us children to carry in for them but we used to stand in our garden and shout out 'Cocoa' as loud as we could and old Tom Jackson would come and collect it.

I left home at Cote Mill in 1971 when I married. John and I have rented the farm at Meysey Hampton ever since from Billy Garne, and keep a small number of the ancient breed of Cotswold sheep with our main flock. Because of the Garne family's long history in saving the breed from extinction I wanted the continuity and to do my part in preserving the bloodline. We are currently in the midst of this terrible foot-and-mouth scourge and it is like sitting on a time bomb, wondering what the next telephone call will bring. I just hope and pray that the end of my farming life won't be imposed on me by such a disaster. It really would be the end of farm life for me. I just couldn't bear to go back to it because the nightmare just wouldn't ever go away.

Margaret Pursch

A Changing Market

The old family home is where Pat and I have brought up our family. My mother's father, John Press, was Master of the Old Berks Foxhounds and that is what brought her family to Lechlade. All the milk and butter and cream from the old dairy here came from our own cows. I was up at five o'clock in the morning to start milking, both here at the back of the dairy and down Mill Lane, where Dad kept the rest of the cattle. When my parents first started the milk round Dad did the delivery on a carrier's bike, two great cans hung on the handlebars, and the milk ladled out into the customer's own jug. You could have as little as a gill measure in those days. Mother bought the first pony we ever had all with threepenny joeys – she saved up every one she could to get Billy. He was a lovely pony – every day, as soon as the cart was loaded, Billy would make off to Jack Ayres's house for his morning toast. Jack regularly put a slice of freshly toasted bread under the door knocker for Billy. We eventually had four ponies to cart the milk floats to get round the deliveries.

When the Manor gardens, which were just over the wall from our back yard, were sold then things changed – we did everything we could to get the sheds mucked out and cleaned to cause the least trouble; but a new housing development did not take kindly to a country dairy as the neighbour. It was not so bad with just the horses, but milking cows in such a close area and, of course, leading off the High Street, didn't fit into the modern image – the way of life started changing rapidly. I had grown up with the old farming ways, and I suppose the wheeling and dealing had always appealed to me – such great old characters you met. You never had anything in writing. Your word was your bond. If you smacked a fellow's hand that was that: the deal had gone through.

After we closed the dairy business we cleaned out all the sheds and stables and I started dealing in furniture – going to auctions and house clearances. I reckon I developed a somewhat keen eye through experience – most of your experience is through bad deals. So I changed my market from dealing with cattle, sheep and pigs to furniture, but the dealers are a different breed from those old livestock dealers – they were great barterers; it was part of the pleasure, striking a bargain. All friendly rivalry. That's what I like to do now, people can come and look round the stock in the yard, barter a bit, strike a deal so as both sides are happy – and off they go.

I remember the furniture sales just along here in the street – probably every month, just opposite Innocent's office. They would stack the stuff from house clearances –most of it bundled up in lots, under the row of trees on the green, and auction it off. It doesn't fit into my idea of country living to have all these things displayed in a shop with artful lighting and little labels with big prices swinging on the chair legs. I like to

Market day at Lechlade, 1928.

Deacon's greengrocers shop in what was their old dairy. The small building on the left with the blocked-up window was probably a gazebo in the Manor grounds.

think I am following on a true old market town tradition.

John Deacon

Talking Shop

My father's first grocery shop was in London Street, at what became the dairy next to Bert Aston's bicycle shop. We moved when I was quite small to the Market Place, taking over from Bobby Green. The premises are very old and were once The Swan Inn. One back window had very thin horn-like panes instead of glass. We lived over the shop and my mother was delighted with the spacious accommodation and particularly when she discovered

that by knocking down a wall at the back we also had a sizeable garden, terribly overgrown – but my parents burnt off the undergrowth and it became somewhere for me and my sisters to play. After the early horse-drawn cart, my father bought a motorcycle and took deliveries out to Eastleach and Southrop in the sidecar.

I went to Farmor's, then passed for grammar school and was doing very well and was looking forward to going on to university to read English and become a teacher, but my father had other plans – which were delayed for a few years when I became of age to serve in the army. His health was not too good so I could not refuse to help him, but I didn't have the initial enthusiasm to become a grocer as he had. He had served a three-year

R.W. Bridges' shop, 1935. From left to right: Sid Tolly, Pauline Bridges, -?-, Tom Boulton.

Dessie Jones in the fruit and veg shop of Bridges. Dessie's family were landlords of The Railway Inn for some seventy years.

apprenticeship, cycling every day from his home at Church Farm, Whelford, to Cirencester. 'Counterhands', as they were known, were very highly regarded and were paid accordingly, but I could only think of how he seemed to spend a whole morning at a time weighing up the rice and sultanas and sugar – sugar was in squared blue paper bags. Biscuits came in large tins and sweets in tall jars – everything had to be weighed up. Tom Gibbard who lived at Victory Villas collected the sacks and crates and boxes and barrels of goods from the railway station and delivered them to us. One of my first duties was to cycle out to Whelford and Kempsford to collect the orders. We were open from 8 a.m. until 8 p.m., but on Saturday nights it was often 10 p.m. My father wouldn't shut up shop until the next door shop closed. Early closing was on Thursday, and, of course, no one opened at all on a Good Friday.

I did follow in my father's footsteps after all – and the shop became R.W. Bridges & Son until I retired.

Dennis Bridges

Robbery In The High Street

Edmonds was the largest department store in this area. People used to say that the whole family and home could be fitted out at Edmonds: there was the men's outfitters, which Vernon Witchell ran for years, ladies' and children's clothing, shoes, haberdashery and household ware, furnishings, and at the bottom of the High Street was their hairdressing salon. I started work there in the office with Olive Cuss when I was just fifteen

and stayed until I was fifty-nine, by which time I was managing the shop.

We used to have a huge round, right out beyond Lechlade to Filkins and Alvescot the one way, over to Bibury and across as far as Driffield – almost into Cirencester the other way. A Miss Ayres started the outride – as it was known – on a bike, then Mr Ash from Horcott went in a large van, collecting orders and delivering to the villages. At that time the majority of villagers had no means of getting to a clothes shop so the country rounds were a real lifeline to them.

The time that we had a robbery caused a tremendous stir in Fairford. Harriett Wall, who was housekeeper for the Samblesons, who kept the post office (which was taken into the Lloyds Bank premises many years ago) heard some noises in the street this par-

Fairford High Street, from Montague House to the Market Place, c. 1896. Powell's shop and Lloyds Bank replaced some old cottages. Edmonds shop is shown with blind out just behind the gas lamp.

ticular night. She pulled her bedroom curtains aside and saw shadowy figures carrying things out of the shop. She rang the police station, which was close by. Ifsobe, as everyone called Sgt Stevens – because he always started off by saying 'If so be I catch you again …' – crept down the other side of the street, saw the parked lorry and, well, as the Magistrates later said, with great presence of mind – he cut the wires of the lorry, then found a coat inside with a card or something with a name and address in. Ifsobe then alerted Joe Cripps, who lived at Laverton House, and Hedley Edmonds, of course, but the couple who were robbing the shop had a getaway plan lined up and went off in Woodwards butchers van, which was parked in Back Lane. They said that Joe Cripps followed them in his pyjamas as far as Wantage and then lost them. Anyway, Ifsobe, of course, had the details and the London police caught them at their home address. They were brought back here for the first hearing. I should think half of Fairford turned out to watch them being taken into court. The little woman that was in the gang, she spat at us because we were all lined up on the pavement. She really was a nasty piece of work. Everyone agreed that Ifsobe had shown that a country copper can outwit a city crook.

Marjorie Heath

The Old George

I was born at The George Inn – in the bedroom above the old sign of St George and the Dragon. It is one of the oldest buildings in Fairford, and we were told that the masons who built the church lived in the cottages that later became The White Hart Inn, and

The George was originally a chantry house for the monks of the church. We had to go through the bar from our living room to go upstairs to bed. My mum and dad never went away on holiday together, they didn't even go away for a honeymoon – it was straight into work when they got married. People didn't go on holidays; the annual George outing to the seaside was such an occasion that there was always a photo taken of the men with the charabanc before they left. My mother always had a spare bed made up, it was something to do with the licence – she said that as we were an inn we couldn't ever refuse a traveller a night's sleep.

Two men always slept in our cellar on a camp bed during the war years – as members of the local fire service they had to be on all night call. The fire engine was stationed in our back yard at the old brew house, my dad was station officer and when he had the call to say there was a fire I had to go round on my bike to get as many other firemen together as quickly as I could. They used to practise with the hand pump every Sunday morning down at the Mill.

My parents had the first skittle alley in the neighbourhood built at The George, at their own expense – then the brewers put up the rent because it was an improved inn! There always seemed to be a lot of real characters around – great individuals, like Bottle Strange and Bertie Wane and Bibury Bill and the old scissor-man, as we called him, we never knew his name but he came round a couple of times a year and sharpened everyone's scissors and grass clippers. He lived in a hut in Pitham Woods, he always seemed a bit tiddly, but he didn't get drunk at our pub, he collected his tipple from Mr Peyman's in a meths bottle.

The old Tudor overhang narrows the Market Square corner yet in all the years we

The George Hotel, c. 1908. The plasterwork was later removed to show the Tudor half-timbering. The George is now Fairford post office.

Fairford's old fire station, 1958. The open-ended barn (now demolished) was at the west end of the old White Hart Inn. The firemen often had to pull the cart themselves – after it was loaded with water pump and (essential) barrel of beer before the horse caught up.

were there we never saw an accident, but an aeroplane being transported on a huge trailer got stuck once just where the half-timbered part of The White Hart juts out. It was stuck for three days and we had to have the roof of our kitchen taken off to get it free.

One evening the soldiers who were stationed here threw all their money to us kids as they left in their army trucks, some left their medals and cap badges with local people – we didn't realize at the time that they were just departing for the D-Day operation – as far as I know, none of them were ever collected.

Phil Hope

Lechlade's old fire station still retains its bell turret. The engine was taken regularly to be washed at the Free Wharf. The building was later used, on occasion, as a temporary mortuary for victims of drowning.

Oh To Be a Farmer's Girl!

My parents took over the tenancy of Waiten Hill Farm when they married: both came from farming families – Dad was at

J.C. Peyman, ironmongers of Fairford in the 1990s – Mrs Clem Peyman and Michael stand at the doorway.

The Grove, Tetbury, and Mum lived at Beverstone Castle. When Richard and I were small children there were thirteen horses on the farm, methods changed and eventually we were left with old Lively – a very misnamed horse if ever there was one, but she was lovely if not lively. Six of us kids could sit in line along her back to amble over the green. We had our pet lambs: Skippy and Joey, and hatched our own eggs. We daren't waste one and Mum showed me how to spit on the shell if it was too dry and rub it in if the chick couldn't get out. She kept ducks as well in the orchard in the early days, it was quite a sight to watch them waddle across the paddock to get to the stream at the bottom. We had to remember to lock them up at night, though. We kept chicken in the old shepherd's hut as well. I took a shotgun to a fox once; the orchard was scattered with dismembered hens, blood spattered all over the grass. I was so upset – the fox just killed for pleasure not for food. I missed, but my dad's wrath was as terrifying. Not on account of the ruthless slaughter of our chickens, but because I had taken a gun to a fox. He was an ardent supporter of the Beaufort Hunt from his Tetbury farming days, and therefore to him the fox was a protected animal, to be dealt with only by the Hunt.

We had two lady evacuees during the wartime: Marguerite Natalia was an opera singer and drove my Dad potty practising her high notes; Miss Pritchard was a teacher and ran her own little school at the top of our house – my brother Richard, and Frank Townsend and some of the other farmers' children were taught by her. Life revolved round the farm: helping Tom Westbury and Fred Hayward, two of our carters, clean the horse brasses – they took such pride in the way the old cart horses were turned out; searching between the nettles and the thick clumps of orchard grass, in the nooks of the old stone walls and the crannies of hay bales collecting eggs in the cool of the evening and helping Mum make up bottles and bottles of cold tea for the threshers and haymakers and harvesters; perfecting the technique of hand milking – the milk was always warm and bubbly. It was an age which was fast coming to a close: women gleaning the harvest fields up Blackford Road, thatched hayricks, stooked corn, fattening up the one-day old chicks we got from Mr Painter's at Quenington, plucking and dressing poultry for Christmas; looking for four-leaved clovers, the smell of apples stored in the loft, ripening and rotting in their collars of newspaper; the thrill of trading surplus to Aubrey Smith to sell as 'touched fruit' in his greengrocer's shop; tying heavy corn sacks round our coat with bag ties to keep warm driving the old Fordson tractor after mastering the throttle and clutch; pulling turnips out of ice-bound mud and the great haul of some seventy or eighty mice that Shirley Pusey, the Nicholls' girls and I had caught in the threshing shed. We put them in a big container and I shut it up in the bike shed by the back door so that I could show the proof of our efforts the next day and maybe, just maybe, get some pocket money reward. The next day dawned – there was the tiniest hole in the bottom of the container – and not one mouse to be seen.

'No daughter of mine goes out to work,' my father said. I had to fight a hard corner to get him to agree to paying me ten shillings a week. 'But you're getting your board and lodging', he argued. However, he did 'equip me out for the job' – with the thickest, heaviest, stiffest, most awful trousers you could imagine and a pair of equally clod-hopping brogues. I was fifteen when I left school – to work on our farm, carrying on with the mucking out and the turnip pulling. He swallowed hard and more than a bit of his inbred snobbery when he learned that I – a farmer's daughter – was marrying a farm worker; a fact somewhat redeemed as Phil was at that time working on Mrs Townsend's farm, not ours!

Liz Hope

Heather's In The High Street

My father and all my ten aunts and uncles were born at the old shop which later became Spaldings' newsagents and, later, where Dessie ran the fruit and veg side as part of Dennis Bridges's shop. The large family soon outgrew the house, of course, and when the row of cottages belonging to the Manor was pulled down next to the old police station, Cam House and the shop to Breakspear House were built. That was where I was born.

My grandfather, Thomas Powell, was a qualified chemist and was known locally as 'Doctor' Powell. I love looking through the little almanacks he presented to his customers and marvel at the range of cure-alls he concocted. One list for 1890, for instance, includes his famous 'Fairford Corn and Wart Cure', 'Effervescing Saline' (for derangements of the liver), and 'Powell's Great Bitter Tonic', 'Powell's Small Liver Pills', and 'Powell's Every

Powell's, drapers of Lechlade.

Powell's drug store and stationers of Fairford, 1948.

Man's Embrocation'. All had testimonials to say how 'excellent, invaluable and celebrated' they proved to be for everything from strengthening the nerves, giving vigour to the frame, settling the wind and curing the rheumatics. Not only did he set out to make everyone better from whatever they might have wrong with them with his pills and potions, but he dealt with all sorts of household and toilet requisites, as they were called – from insect powder to distilled essences ranging in perfume from white roses to 'new mown hay'. His list of sundry medical requisites was extensive – from bunion plasters to artificial limbs, sea-going medicine chests to fumigating paper to horse hair gloves, though, goodness knows what they were for! He really developed the stationery side, too, and even published small booklets, as well as selling fishing tackle.

Charles Powell, the eldest son took over the business – he was the great photographer of the family and I still have a letter sent from Balmoral Castle thanking Aunt Louise Powell for the photograph he sent to Queen Mary when she visited the church in 1922. After Charles died, my father, A.E. Powell – but always known as Bert – came into the business. Two of my uncles became drapers – Tom Powell had the last big drapery at Lechlade, and Uncle Harry had the draper's shop here in the High Street, next to the Little Alley. I remember we always joined the family on Boxing Day to watch the old mummers play there.

I kept the old name when I took over from my parents and I remember how the Americans during the wartime expected to have soda fountains in our 'drug store'. It was good to carry on the family tradition into and beyond a century, and proudly boast the first 'circulating library' here, but I enjoyed it more as a way of life than concentrating on being a financial success – having a bottle of sherry under the counter for my regular customers at Christmas was much more fun. I remember being overawed at the introduction of artificial snow in a can and proudly demonstrated how effective it was to Mrs Sid Perry. 'Look, look' I urged her – squirting like fury at a sheet of paper I was holding up; she looked, and I looked, there was nothing on it. I gave it all the squirt I could and looked round as she squealed – in what I thought was amazement, only to find her covered from head to toe in white foam – a perfect picture of Mrs Santa.

Heather Shuttlewood

Hope At Heather's

We took over Powell's newsagent and stationer's shop in 1976 from Heather – her family had been there for so long everybody called it Heather's, then eventually it became known as Liz and Phil's. We ran it very much on the same lines as Heather had, but eventually we had to change our opening times to meet modern demands, so we were open all through the day from 6 a.m. seven days a week. For years we fought against opening on a Sunday, but had to in the end to survive in business, but we felt uncomfortable, even embarrassed, right opposite the church and trying to teach established values to our two children.

Local shops depend on local support. We never ceased to be amazed by some of the

Phil and Liz Hope sharing a joke with customers in their High Street shop.

The Trout Inn, 1902 – the last pub on leaving Lechlade on the Faringdon Road.

remarks made to us. One woman, whom we knew for certain had lived here for at least ten years, said 'oh, I didn't know you sold cards'; we told her we reckoned we had the greatest range anywhere – she bought a stamp. Our pet hate phrase was: 'I've been everywhere in Cirencester, I don't suppose you stock it.' Invariably we did, and had, for years. Time and again we would be asked to 'read the words, dear, I've forgotten my glasses' – in a number of cases we realized that a number of these customers could neither read nor write.

The purpose for buying cards was a constant revelation: after reading out the words in one particular card, the lady said 'oh, I don't think my budgie would like those words – he is sending the card to a friend's budgie, you see'. Perhaps the unique one in our twenty-one years at the shop was the woman who wanted every one of the jokey cards – our entire stock. We told her it came to a total of over £60 and made some remark about she must have a lot of friends. 'I'm not sending these to anyone,' she snorted, 'I am getting them to throw away, so that you stop selling this kind of card.' Needless to say we persuaded her that it would rather defeat the object, we would only have to replenish the stock to meet the demands of other customers!

Phil and Liz Hope

The Trout

I understand the original inn dates back to about 1220 as part of the priory, and was known as The Sign of St John the Baptist

The Railway Inn, c. 1900, with landlord John Kibblewhite – the last pub on leaving Fairford on the Lechlade Road.

Derek Radway, the last of the Fairford family bakers.

Head. It is certainly on a very historic site at St John's Bridge which is said to have been built in stone by the monks in 1217 to replace an earlier wooden one. The monks are reputed to have distilled their own Benedictine over the old fireplace in the Anglers Bar and records speak of fish swimming in this old oak-beamed room during the high floods of 1903. The ancient fishing rights are vested in the landlord, and these are said to have been granted by Royal Charter to the brothers of the priory, including 'a fishery of 200 eels less 25'. The fishery rights extend for two miles of the Thames to Inglesham and I let them out to an angling club. What a wealth of old tales there must be locked in these old walls!

Bob Warren

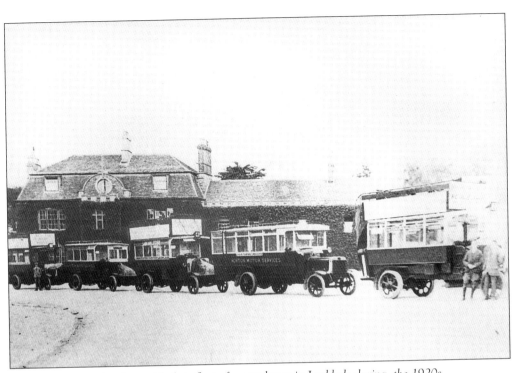

The three Norton brothers with their fleet of motor buses in Lechlade during the 1920s.

Young's garage, Lechlade (now the Christmas shop), with Trixie Yarnold. M. Youngs ran an early steam-driven bus service to Cirencester in Edwardian times.

CHAPTER 7

High Days, Holidays and Pastimes

Fairford Town Band, 1906.

Come, Listen To The Band

That's what Mr Cook said, 'Come in and listen instead of sitting outside.' He had seen me sitting on the stone wall outside the infant school. My brother, Fred, was in the band and I would go down and listen to them all practising. I had always been interested in music and had piano lessons with Mrs

Chivers who lived down the bottom of the alley, then I went to Peggy Bridges for a while – well, that gave me enough confidence to go up the Polish camp and play with their little orchestra. I remember looking forward to playing some Polish music, but they wanted me to play 'Come Back to Sorrento'. Anyway, Mr Cook taught me to play the tenor horn and I became the first female

Fairford Silver Band rehearsing for their TV role.

member of Fairford Silver Band. We had to be measured for new uniforms and I was so embarrassed when the tailor ran the tape measure round me. There were a lot of events – whist drives and concerts – put on to raise the money for the cost of the uniform. I think the total was £170 – and there must have been something like twenty-five in the band at that time.

Three years ago we had another new uniform – very snazzy green jackets with black collars and cuffs. These jackets cost £145 each. Like most other places, our numbers have dwindled, there are only fourteen of us now so it is difficult to meet all the demands – people do like band music for their fêtes and functions, it's part of our tradition. We had our spot of national fame a couple of years ago when we had to play for a village fête scene of *Forgotten*, a television thriller starring Amanda Burton. Our eye-catching jackets added just the right amount of colour

to the village green, they said. We really enjoyed it, but it was odd having to mime to a recording of our own playing.

It would be nice to think that with such a long history we could increase the number of players by the time we reach our centenary. Of course, most of the men were called up for the First World War and the instruments and uniforms were stored in Park House cellars. It was 1920 before the band started up again and they went on to win several major contests and became Fairford Prize Band. Mr A.J. Cook became band master in 1935 and completed fifty years as an active bandsman. Mr Bert Cuss followed him, he had been in the band since the end of the First World War, then Alfie Cook took over. Cecil Voaden is our present band master – and, like Mr Cook when I first joined, Cecil will teach anyone who is interested to play. Both my sons, Philip and Christopher, were members of our band until their careers took them away from Fairford – my dad used to be secretary at one time, so we have been very involved as a family – I still am. Half a century on, and still blowing my own trumpet, you might say!

Mary Vizor

Making Music

My parents were paying a shilling a week for violin lessons with Mr Mate the butcher and then it went up to half a crown when I 'graduated' to tuition with a Mr DeTurnerville from Swindon along with Joan Collier and Geoff Fullock, practising in Collier's the baker's big back room. I made it to second violin in Mr Mate's little orchestra, but I really wanted to play the piano like my sister Janet – but my mum kept it locked up. When I had saved up £3 10s from taking people out in the boats I sent away for a mandolin-banjo, much to my Dad's amusement, and as it was similar to the violin I got on really well with it. It had much more get-up-and-go and I used to get asked to David Moulden's home at Fyfield quite often. David could play the banjo really well so it was good fun playing together – his uncle, George Morley from Fairford was an excellent player and played in concerts.

Peggy Cooper

Fairford Carnival

Having spent much of my early childhood at Fairford Park with my godparents, Colonel and Mrs Palmer, I soon realized that this little Cotswold town was the seat of two great industries: the fat stock show and the carnival. Having been designated the task of judging the latter, I almost feel that I should have opted for the former, for Mrs Gordon Lennox and I have had a terribly hard job. I know that in the months preceding the carnival all the town has taken to its feet because everything on wheels has been locked away and guarded against spies while you beaver away in the barns transforming the Geaches' and Gantletts' and Cole's and Iles's hay-waggons into these incredible vehicular visions.

Fairford Carnival has grown over the years to become, and I quote, 'the greatest show in the West of England' – from its beginnings as a cycle carnival, followed by one of those glorious old social gatherings of Victorian times – 'A Smoker' – held at The Bull. Today, we have all kinds of delights and the usual firework display. Mr Horace Baldwin has attracted no less than thirty-two bands to compete in the contest. I wonder whether Colonel Palmer realizes that he is going to have 660 to tea! As you know, it has always been his principle to entertain the bandsmen to tea on carnival day. No, Colonel Bertie, it is of no use you signalling across to Mrs Gantlett for I have it on good authority that she and her 200 helpers have just served the five thousandth tea. Fairford shops have been cleaned right out of food and all available supplies have been borne in by gallant messengers all afternoon from Lechlade and Poulton.

The whole of Fairford has obviously laboured long and lovingly to make this year of 1937 a memorable one – a most fitting tribute for the Golden Jubilee of Fairford Cottage Hospital – the fund-raising object of all these carnivals. I have never enjoyed myself more, I hope you feel the same. Good luck to Fairford.

David Niven
(From the recording made for the son et
lumière of 1978)

David Niven presenting first prize to Melba Tozer at Fairford Carnival.

WILTS AND GLOUCESTERSHIRE STANDARD, SA

Photos : W. Dennis Moss, Cirencester, and Bert Powell, Fairford.

Mrs Gordon Lennox and Mr. David Niven, the well-known film actor (who has lived in Cirencester and Fairford), two of the judges, awarding first prize to Melba Tozer.

A Famous Day At The Carnival

The photograph of me with David Niven is my one claim to fame, although at the time I was not really aware of its importance. Fairford Carnival was such an exciting event in our young lives. It took weeks of preparation and the entries were always worked on in the utmost secrecy. One year I went as Queen of Hearts and had great difficulty in keeping the tarts on the tray.

The entertainment in the ring was always very good. I once watched the household cavalry arrive on a special train to take part. My father was always busy helping to run the band contest, so we didn't see him until the evening then he took us to the fair, with the power supplied to the rides by the huge steam engines.

Melba Barnfield

Through The Generations

It is rather nice to have a visual link back to one's family; the wrought iron railings on the Mill Bridge were made at my great-grandfather's forge at Waterloo House and you can still see the name, E.B. Chew on their base – he was Edgar Buxton Chew. My grandfather had the shop next to R.W. Bridges; also dealing in grocery, provisions, wine and spirits. He used to talk about old Dicky Watts, a tiny figure of a man who

Edgar Buxton Chew outside Waterloo House, where he had a forge works, with his daughters.

did deliveries with his donkey cart, and did all kinds of carrier jobs – generally, a very useful person to have around.

My mother went to Miss Starkey's private school in the Croft, and later taught there, and that is where I had my first schooling. Miss Starkey was a very tall, austere lady. We had to stand in a long line to repeat our times-tables, she was a great advocate of the learning by rote system. The old tortoise stove, which the pupils had to keep charged up with coke, had chronic congestion problems. Sometimes we had to put something in it which exploded to clear the flue, so we learnt some basic element of combustion along with the Scriptures, with which she was much taken, and how to endure the rash of splinters on the seats of the wooden

desk benches. In later years I returned to the old Croft School to teach music, and my mother held a small kindergarten school here at Redlands House.

Grandfather was very involved with community affairs and was a founder member of the Cycle Carnival committee the forerunner of the famous Fairford Carnival and so, of course, I was annually exhibited in what ever fancy dress Mother devised. Through the years I stoically processed with the rest of Fairford: as Miss Muffet, with a shoulder-clinging toy spider; the Queen of Hearts with the obligatory tray of tarts; a wimple-hatted Plantagenet lady and a very imaginative invention as a paintbox – my green dress even had a loop on the back by which to hang up the said paintbox which was displayed in glowing

Snow clearance outside E.B. Chew's ironmonger's shop (now part of Coln Gallery), c. 1920.

Dicky Watts (postilion rider to Queen Adelaide), with his donkey cart, talks to Mr Chew outside his grocer's shop (now David Atherton's family butcher's shop) in the Market Place.

Dennis and Peggy Bridges with their first prize and champion entry in the Fairford Carnival of 1954.

colours down the front when I held back the lid. I must admit I did not appreciate the work that Mother put into these creations at the time that I was growing up and conscious of being on public display – but it was traditional, and a huge community event which largely financed the running of our cottage hospital.

There was tremendous secrecy about the entries: every shop and organization decorated a float, originally horse-drawn farm carts and wagons and then later cars and motorcycles were allowed to enter as decorated vehicles. When the carnival was revived after the war Dennis was very involved organising the great band contest and we decided to make our entry the bandstand. We made thousands of crepe paper flowers all through the winter and

worked in the barn next to The Railway Inn. Just before the great day an overnight downpour had leaked through the barn roof and ruined a great part of our decoration. We were up practically all night frantically making more crepe flowers. What a drama, but we won first and champion prizes, and the silver cup for the best exhibit in the carnival of 1954.

Peggy Bridges

One Of Isaac's Disciples

John Taylor, the headmaster of Farmor's School published this verse as my grandfather's obituary.

'The last of the old time fisherman
Has crossed to the other shore.
Never again will he wield the rod
Nor cast a fly any more.
Mr Powell was very well known
To fishermen far and near,
Affectionately styled 'the Doctor',
As a fisher he had no peer.
Merry and jolly in his prime,
With quips and jokes made free,
Made many records of lusty trout,
Keen disciple of 'Old Isaac' he.
No more prognosticate the time
When May fly'd be on the scene,
No more he'll cast the yellow dun
Or drakes of grey and green.
By many he'll be remembered
When fly is up on the Coln,
His ready advice, a memory dear,
No more he'll cast on his own.'

Heather Shuttlewood

'Dr' Charles Powell fishing in the Coln: his diary records his total catch in one week in 1880 as 22 brace weighing 56lb.

A Teenager's Tight Line

I was absolutely fishing mad and spent much of my youth regularly filling my wellies with water from the Horcott gravel pits. I made a map of what was grandly called The Lakes and plotted on it my every catch. I used to gaze in awe at the stuffed trout in its glass case in The Bull but was fascinated by the folklore surrounding pike-fishing and kept records of the ones I caught. This particular evening I hadn't set out to do much fishing, but couldn't resist running down to where the scout hut is now and just as it was getting dusk had this sudden bite. It was the culmination of an experiment by which I thought that if I used a bigger bait I could catch a bigger fish, my pals had ridiculed the idea, but there it was – it felt like a crocodile

on the end of the line and I didn't have a landing net with me. I couldn't manage to carry the pike home as well as my tackle, so I buried it under a load of weed on the bank.

It was a beauty and weighed in at 18lb 2ozs. I so badly wanted to preserve it, but couldn't afford a taxidermist. I had read that the great Jardin had made plaster casts of his species, and so I asked Dad to set it in a plaster cast. He did. It was done by the time I got home from school the next day. He had done it as a surprise, but all I could think of was the very straight back, and I had studied pike for so long that I knew that when they are resting their back is slightly arched. However, I was glad that he hadn't got the mouth open as you often see them – quite

Andrew Jones reminiscing with his father, Ralph, with the cast model of the pike he caught at the age of sixteen.

unnatural. I was elevated to the realms of fishing folklore among my contemporaries for a while, they were all invited to come and view and ooh and aah at it. We had to chip the mould away because of so many intricate bits on the fish, then I painted it and preserved it for all time. After that I caught one pike that had another pike inside it that had a perch inside it – but that's another tale.

Andrew Jones

England's Finest Battles

I have been cricket crazy since I can remember, and am still treasurer of the Lechlade Cricket Club. From all the records we can find it looks as though cricket has been played on the Manor grounds for well over a hundred years. A document dated 1904 describes the Cricket and Tennis Clubs as having sole use of: 'That piece of pasture land situated in 'Englands' in the Parish of Lechlade, measuring three acres and thirty perches, or thereabouts, at a yearly rent of £7 16s. 4d. Also the tenants shall have peaceable and quiet possession of the said land during the tenancy.'

Peaceable and quiet? Well, the battles fought there over the years have been in the best cricketing tradition; I remember once, back in the fifties, we had a West Indian member – Bert Cooper, and like his fellow countrymen Bert took the game very

Lechlade Cricket Club, 1959. From left to right, back row: R. Archer, M. Sparkes, G. Cox, J. Rae, B. Archer, D. Tombs, G. Moreing, T. Powell. Third row: I. Pettifer, C. Hayhurst France, Mrs Skull, Mrs Cox, Mrs Wise, Mrs Keep (the tea ladies), F. Keep, J. Hudson. Second row: J. Archer, R. Land, J. Freeth, A. Skull, E. Parker, L. Cox, G. Oakley. Front row: G. Brooks, J. Deacon, R. Hayden, B. Sparkes.

seriously. He was partnering John Deacon at the wicket. Bert drove the ball and they ran one. Bert turned to go for the second. John, wily judge of all things cricket, held up his hand. 'Naw, bide thar', he shouted. Bert stopped in his tracks, out of his ground. John bid him again to 'bide thar'. Bert was rooted to the spot and the bails were whipped off. The look of bewilderment on poor Bert's face was a picture as he walked off asking 'What did he say?' John Freeth tried to explain, but in our Gloucestershire dialect which left Bert even more mystified. He left us soon after to join Swindon Caribbeans – where he could, no doubt, understand the local lingo better!

The old thatched pavilion was burnt to the ground during the time that bigger battles 'stopped play' at Lechlade. It was due to an immense effort and dedication that funds were raised to buy a replacement sectional hut for starting again in 1947. Cricket teas of yore were taken at The Trout Inn: the long white cloth-covered tables, with jam jars filled with wild flowers, and, pride of place, amid the plates of sandwiches, was Jimmy Gearing's famous lardy cakes. Apart from being the most wonderful lardies, we reckon, in the West

Fairford Scouts Football Club, 1935. Centre back: Mr Harrison and Mr Aubrey Smith. From left to right, standing: Eric Jefferies, Les Grant, Jack Stevens, Ted Browning, Percy Wall, Charlie Indge, Jim Swinford, Jim Wall. Front row: Len Godding, George Egerton, Les Radway, Sid Radway, George Marks.

Country, I took more than a bit of pride in the fact that as Sid Gearing was my uncle by marriage, and we lived in the cottage alongside the bakery, I often helped make them in school holidays. I was allowed to weigh out the dough, then roll it out, spread the lard and sugar and dried fruit over then fold and roll it again. This was repeated a number of times before the lardy was put in the tin, then a diamond pattern was marked out on top and that made it lovely and crispy. I was not 'qualified' to shape the loaves, though. Our house was permeated with the smell of freshly baked bread. The bakery was always busy because the Gearing brothers had to go back in the evening to knead the dough and put in the great troughs to rise. Later on, I helped with

the deliveries, too, the bread round went out as far as Kelmscott and Kempsford and Whelford as well as locally in the town on the errand boy's bike.

The post-war pavilion eventually beat our wonderful tea ladies into complaints about sharing the kitchen with the field mice, the roof was noticeably suffering from middle-age sag, priming the pump on the well for water was becoming a bit tedious and it was taking a brave man to enter what was serving us as 'the gents'. More feverish fund-raising and even more dedicated man-power resulted in our having a new pavilion opened in 1972 by Sister Dominique, the Mother Superior of the Convent.

Lechlade near Fairford, or Fairford near Lechlade? The definition is decided on our

River Race in the Coln between the Mill and Town Bridges as part of Fairford's Coronation celebrations in 1952: Dr Michael Veale (on left), -?-, and Miss Norman are the gallant contestants.

England's hallowed green. The neighbourly small market town rivalry dates back to the earliest cricket days. I remember being told the tale of one of our annual 'blood' matches against Fairford when Jimmy Griffin, fishmonger of this parish, was umpire and his l.b.w. decision queried by a Fairford batsman. 'I was never out you know, Jim,' he appealed. Jim replied, 'If you don't believe it, look in the *Wilts and Glos* next week.'

Ray Hayden

West of England Swimming and Diving championships at Lechlade, c. 1910.

Lt-Gen. Sir Robert Baden Powell inspects the Lechlade Scouts in 1916.

Fairford Cubs, 1975.

Lechlade Swimming Club: the annual August Bank Holiday Water Carnival was held from 1903 to 1935.

Crowds throng Mill Lane for the Jubilee River Race of 1977.

CHAPTER 8
Memorable Folk and Feats

Prince Erik and his father, the King of Denmark, at Park Farm, Fairford.

The Student Prince

We have the ancestral Iles forever watching us from their sepia photographs that we have in our farmhouse, and what a fascinating tale there must be to be told behind that collection. Unfortunately, the time that Prince Erik of Denmark was sent to Park Farm as a student to learn farming from grandfather Ken Iles has left little more than a vague childhood memory recalled by Aunt Janet, who said that they were so young at the time they didn't accord him the deference adults would have. They rather thought of the Prince as a sort of fun nurse maid who pushed them around the garden.

Bob And Jenny Iles

Author's note

'Our man' from *The Times* was sent to Fairford to report on the progress of Prince Erik on an English farm, only to find the royal student in 'that time-honoured educational establishment, The Bull, showing the locals how to play snooker with a fishing rod and a handful of tomatoes!

Witch, Reaper Or Gypsy

When I was about ten years old I chose to write about Betty's grave for my school work on places of interest in our area. I said that if you enquire of the local inhabitants about this grave – a simple mound on the crossroads along the back road from Fairford to Cirencester – you will be told that Betty was a poor woman who worked for the farmer who owned the field close by. One harvest time the labourers all refused for some reason to work for this farmer. The field was full of ripe golden corn which Betty hated to see go to waste. She took a sickle and single-handed cut down the whole field of corn, but collapsed and died as she left the field when her work was done.

Marion Nash

Author's note

The origin of Betty's Grave is shrouded in mystery and folklore: tales abound as to why she was buried at a crossroads – the favoured spot often for depositing suicides and witches; that Betty was a witch who was tried and died so many times that the story lacks credence is, nevertheless, still a favoured explanation. Sightings of a ghostly girl in the vicinity have been reported within living memory. That Betty lived is certain: Betty was Elizabeth Bastoe of Poulton; that she died is obvious – but how many times and how is not – but she has been accorded the distinction of official recognition on the Ordnance Survey map and as a postal address. It is the floral tributes that appear mysteriously on the simple mound from time to time that are as enigmatic as the circumstance of it being there:

'Betty dear, my love,
You've turned to grass;
I've travelled along the road and I'm weary
Now I'll pay my best regards, old deary.'

The message tied to a jam jar of bright yellow daffodils one morning sparked off the long held belief that it is travelling folk who pay 'best regards'. Letters to the editor of the *Wilts and Gloucestershire Standard* have raised the question again – who was Betty, who was she?

It Must Be Kept Up

Well, it was all a long time ago, wasn't it. I believe it was in 1777 that Betty was buried there at the crossroads. There was a cross there at one time, but over the years that has disappeared, but no, I have never seen anyone put flowers on her grave, most folk think it's the gypsies, well strangers, anyway, although some believe it is us that live close by. There are a lot of tales told about her, but I've always understood Betty took on a wager to mow a field in a day, and she died from exhaustion and was buried at the spot where she died. No, I've never put any flowers there, but I do mow it – I have since 1948. I am eighty-six now and still do it voluntarily. I don't know who will do it when I'm gone. But I like to see it tidy. It must be kept up – that is what Mr Idiens said. He was the surveyor when I worked for the council. And I do. I'll keep it up as long as I can.

Jack Tugwell

Author's Note

Joan Idiens, also a close neighbour, said 'That sounds just the sort of thing my father would have said: that Betty's grave should be kept up, and Jack certainly does that – he mows the complete corner, it is a credit to him. I am sure my father could not have envisaged the increase of traffic that uses this road now, it used to be so quiet. Unfortunately, the traffic has eroded the grass verge. No, I have never seen anyone put flowers on the grave. It could well be local people, just to keep up the tradition. The popular story in the paper now is that Betty was a gypsy princess, but we don't see the old Romanies on the road these days, although there are gypsy-type caravans to be seen from time to time in the area. I don't suppose we shall ever know the truth behind all the tales. It is a mystery spot – it is somehow nice for it to remain a mystery.'

Ethel Bluett

My first introduction to Lechlade was in the hot summers of 1936 to 1938. My father had bought three fields and we spent very enjoyable camping holidays by the river. We later moved to a house on the edge of the fields, and my parents took 'a great risk' in sending me to the Catholic Convent. I returned to Lechlade after I was widowed and Miss Bluett offered accommodation to me and my two very young sons in her cottage in Sherborne Street.

Ethel Bluett was a remnant of Victoriana, she loved children but was a strict disciplinarian and was a formidable figure in full-length voluminous skirts; she created quite a picture when she rowed boatloads of scrubby little boys in the widest boat she could hire to give them a river treat. She stuck to a very rigid schedule – a characteristic she perhaps inherited from her military father. Sundays followed a set pattern: 8 a.m. Holy Communion, back home to breakfast; then Sunday classes which she held for small groups of children, illustrating stories from the Old Testament with her puppet theatre – which, no doubt, she had made herself. She maintained all the best stories were in the Old Testament and Christianity came much earlier and in a more primitive manner than we think. Early afternoon she caught the bus to Oxford to visit her nieces.

A truly hale and hearty lady, Miss Bluett walked everywhere. She kept the front door of her cottage open summer and winter, there was no central heating. I remember on one of those damp and misty mornings to which Lechlade seems particularly prone, after making my bed with my gloves on I closed my bedroom window. 'My dear,' she said, on my return from teaching all day, 'I think you inadvertently closed your window this morning, so I opened it for you'. She was extremely public-spirited and leapt at the opportunity of hauling the tin bath from the back wall in front of the fire with just the regulated depth of water during one of the many unexplained water shortages which we had to endure. Everyone else seemed to be wallowing in more comfortable depths with impunity. She had a fund of stories and must have been one of the last of the great ballad exponents.

We later moved to Thames Cottage by St Lawrence's School, but I changed the name to Dove Cottage when I discovered from Mr Innocent's sales particulars that it had formerly been a small beerhouse, Dove Inn, used by the boatmen, with an old track from the cottage down to the river.

June Howell

Emily Golding

Some summers when we had people to stay at Bridge House, Janet and I had to go to old Great-Cousin Emily Golding. It was very claustrophobic in her small cottage in Sherborne Street after our big house. Emily was a dear old lady but she had a very bad speech impediment. We were told that when she was seventeen years old she worked up at the Round House and one evening fell down a step whilst carrying a tray of best china. It so frightened her that she lost her power of speech for ages and then it only partially returned, so people had difficulty in understanding her, but we kids were brought up with it and could make out most of what she said. She would come up to tea at four o'clock nearly every day during the war. She made a habit of calling on a round of friends at breakfast, dinner and supper times and so was able to sell her rations.

Peggy Cooper

Author's Note

My mother told my brother and I that if we told a lie in the churchyard we would be 'struck like poor Emily'. As we had to go through the churchyard to school, we would hurry along Shelley's Walk with our lips tightly pursed for fear of letting any little untruth inadvertently slip. It was perhaps the most graphic of the many country beliefs in swift and awful retribution and was on par with not whistling at the moon or making funny faces in case the wind changed and we would be stuck like it!

Abbey At The Hall

Morgan Hall is very much home to me, but I have always been acutely conscious of the fact that it has been home to many interesting people dating back to the reign of Henry Tudor. I really feel emotions of pride and a deep sense of responsibility, almost as though I am a mere custodian of its heritage and I have constantly worked on retaining and restoring the basic fabric to preserve its outstanding features – it is a convivial country house with rooms of exquisite proportions, but it has to be manageable and personalized as a family home. There is a great presence in the house – there is an aura of something special, but never negative or nasty. As would be expected, Morgan Hall has its reputed ghost – the ubiquitous grey lady in the parkland. I have never seen her, but there is a strong element of sound and atmosphere which cannot be readily explained, but I find the reality much more interesting: the tangible evidence of life here in the past, such as old Burford trade tokens in the plasterwork and a huge debris bottle bank all found during renovation work here.

The garden is important to me, too, and it is thrilling to have the ha-ha intact edging the parkland. I am endeavouring to plant trees for future generations to enjoy and I am happy for people to walk the top end of the park as a local amenity and in its way is a continuity of the contribution the Walter Jones family made to the community and I like to envisage all the activity at Morgan Hall in the time that the Abbeys were here. Edwin Abbey was a celebrated American artist who did much of his famous work here from 1890 for the last twenty years of his life. He had the largest studio in England – and quite possibly the largest in the whole of Europe –

Edwin Abbey's XI on the cricket field at Morgan Hall, 1903. From left to right, standing: Arnesby Brown, Henry Ford, Gerald Chown, D. Luard, Arthur Studd, Reginald Bloomfield, G. Hillyard Swinstead. Seated: G. Gascoign, Edwin Abbey, Hon. Walter Jones, Mrs Gertrude Abbey, L. Nightingale.

Photograph taken by Edwin Abbey, of Nora (later Evans) held by her mother, Bessie Keylock, 1902, from which he used the baby's arms as a model in his famous mural, The Holy Grail.

huge: 64ft x 40ft x 25ft. After his death, Gertrude, his wife, had it pulled down and the spot reverted again to the kitchen garden. I would love to have seen him working, in his old soft felt hat, with a hole in the crown for ventilation and the brim pulled well down to shade his eyes, and often singing some old ballad. He was fascinated with English cricket and founded the Artists' Cricket Club in 1898, he held a week-long cricket festival of his own every summer. Think of all those great artists and writers coming to stay at Morgan Hall and playing cricket in the parkland, and what fascinating conversations they must have had as they sat over their evening meal.

There were also many nobles of the day who came here for sittings for Abbey's Coronation picture of Edward VII, a great number of them would have come down by train, I suppose. It is said that Abbey did not appreciate the accolade this royal commission accorded him – simply because he loved

Jim Luce riding his bike on the frozen Thames in 1963.

to work and live in complete freedom – but he obviously could not refuse the King's command, so was able to add 'court painter' to his already prestigious portfolio. What is so wonderful is that Abbey often used local people as models for his studies. He had the most incredible wardrobe of historical costumes, Mrs Abbey supervised the making of many of them here, so local seamstresses would have been used too. Singer Sargent joined the Abbeys in 1891 and worked with him on the mammoth Holy Grail frieze for the Capitol building in Washington, again, local people were invited to act as models.

What a way to perpetuate the characteristics of a place and its people – albeit in an allegorical format in so many of the great artist's work: one of St Mary's church windows as an illustration for *The Quiet Life*, the yard of Bridge House at Lechlade as a background in Goldsmith's *The Deserted Village*, and also for that book – a corner of the drawing room at Morgan Hall – his one time home, now, very happily, mine.

Barry Fenby

Cycling On The Thames

We had always heard about the 'Big Freeze' when it was said there was an ox roast on the Thames, but that was a couple of hundred years ago – in the history books. I never expected anything like that sort of winter in my lifetime, but I heard that the Thames was frozen right over, so I went off on my bike to see. Well, I saw our local policeman walk across from one bank to the other; he was a big fellow and someone told me he weighed eighteen stone, so I thought that if the ice took his weight I would try it on my bike. I was amazed how smooth it was to ride on the iced-up river,

I didn't wobble at all and carried on right down the middle of the river, under the Ha'penny Pike Bridge and through the other side; then there was a great splintering noise and the ice cracked right across just a few yards behind me – that made me wobble a bit, especially as I thought at that moment, 'Help, I can't swim'. By then there was quite a gathering of people on the banks; I remember Mrs Titchener – Bert's wife – she was absolutely flabbergasted that I was riding on the river and took several photos. Then a few more people joined in, one or two more on bikes, others slipping and sliding about and – a couple on proper ice -skates – but further upriver from where I had just come from.

That is certainly a date I shall remember: 5 February 1963. The next day the ice was under water. Only a few months ago a little group of children was coming from the school and they pointed to me and shouted out: 'there he is, there's the man that rode his bike on the river'. I asked them how they knew about it, it was so long ago and they said they had been told about it in their local history lesson: I never thought I would be known to be part of Lechlade history.

Jim Luce

No Slip Up

On the historic day when the Thames was frozen enough for us to walk across, I joined in although I was carrying our youngest son, John at the time. It was a bit precarious, although, as a doctor, I knew what to do if he decided to come earlier than expected, but I did make the return trip a bit quicker because I did not want him born 'on the other side'. But all was well and he is Gloucestershire-born, so all county honour preserved!

Sheila Stephens

Meg Remembers

I grew up living above and behind our butcher's shop in London Street, my father and uncle carried on the business which had been Gran'pa Perry's and deliveries were still by horse and cart until we had our first van in 1934. Gran'ma Perry was Sam Burge's daughter – he was a master saddler whose shop was just inside Back Lane at Byways.

I was fascinated by the old girls who lived in the tiny cottages down the alley from the shop: Fanny Simms was always so immaculate, her hair neatly pinned in a top knot and her long apron was always snowy white, Dad said she was the best poultry dresser he ever had. I was scared stiff of her mother, although she never spoke to me, she would sit in her old Windsor chair by the cooking range and just look at me. Hannah Watts, who lived next door, was a case and a bit; I used to watch her from my bedroom window when she would stand out by her well at the back cleaning her teeth, dressed only in her corsets. She was the exact opposite to fussy Fanny, but I loved to get into her cottage and she would give me a great chunk of crusty new bread with lashings of butter on it. My mother complained that it would spoil my appetite for dinner. 'Ah! The little maid likes it, Mary,' old Hannah would say – and I did.

Old Jack Ryman, the dairyman, always called me his little maid, too. I remember once I fell into a great bed of nettles in the field behind us, where the ponies were kept. He picked me up, grabbed a handful of dock leaves, spit on them and pressed them against the stinging blisters – that's an old-fashioned remedy, but it works. Bert Aston's bike shop between us and the dairy was hung all around and piled up with spares and bits, but he could always find exactly the right thing for you; his wife was a wonderful dressmaker.

The cottagers used their garden wells as a sort of fridge, lowering their can of milk, perhaps a parcel of butter and any bit of meat they could afford, wrapped in muslin, in a bucket to just above the water level to keep cool in the summertime.

My memories of Christmas time was of our kitchen table – a long deal scrubbed top table – laden for at least two weeks with tongues and hams. The Perry brothers' pickling recipes were dead secret, known only to them, as was their famous sausages – they made mountains of sausages in what we called the cellar, on account of the thatched building where all this went on at the back being down three steps. It was wonderfully cool, and as the shop faced north it never got the sun through the windows. Meat couldn't have been fresher, it was all slaughtered on the premises at the back – Woodwards further up the street had their own slaughterhouse, too, in the Back Lane.

I used to help with cleaning piles of chitterlings – Dad earned his living that way, so he didn't think anything of me learning how to do those sorts of jobs as well. During the wartime, when the men were away in the services, I did the deliveries on the old carrier bike with its butcher boy wicker baskets. Every night the butcher's block was sprinkled with sawdust, scrubbed white with a wire brush and everything scalded in boiling soda water – nothing could survive that, we never heard about food poisoning or anything like that in those days.

Meg Perry

Meg Perry, aged four, 'riding' the Perry brothers' first delivery motor.

Piano Lessons

Miss Virginia Du Plat Taylor was her full name, 'Ginnie' to close friends and family, and certainly a most eccentric and interesting person. Quite petite, short bobbed hair pulled back and secured with hair combs, wonderful bushy eyebrows above her spectacles and protruding teeth – I viewed all these physical aspects with the curiosity of a nine-year-old during each of the forty-minute piano lessons I had in her home at Lakeside. Usually the lessons were on Saturday mornings, but occasionally they were after school – teatime took on a completely new meaning after I had met Miss Du Plat Taylor. She drank China tea, infused with a silver spoon – terribly sophisticated to my young eyes – she was allergic to yeast so ate special bread

125

Katherine Mitchell teaching Samuel, Thomas and Christopher an exercise she learnt from Miss Du Plat Taylor.

made from soya flour spread with WI home-made jam; her preference was for rosehip and rhubarb! The elegance of the afternoon tea was somewhat marred by the mesh-covered plate of tripe sitting on the sideboard. I often wondered whether it was in readiness for her dinner or the cat's supper – it certainly left an indelible impression on my memory, mainly because of the pungent smell which pervaded the house.

Moffat, the large tabby cat, became a significant part of my lessons and at times his escapades would disrupt them completely. The most dramatic time was while I was struggling with my scales when suddenly Miss Taylor leapt up from her seat and shrieked. Moffat had brought in a mouse and was anxious to show his trophy to us, but the mouse escaped Moffat's grip and was scut-tling round the room. Miss Taylor enlisted my help and both armed with family-size yoghurt pots we dived and lunged at the poor little thing, getting in each other's and Moffat's way. Finally, the mouse had enough and took refuge – running up the leg of Miss Taylor's decidedly baggy trousers. More shrieks, another escape – both for the luck-less mouse and for me from the scheduled scales and arpeggios.

Apart from the cat and mouse episode, Miss Taylor taught me so much that I have never forgotten – an excellent teacher, she had been a pupil of Gustav Holst. I under-stood she had once been a nun. She was certainly a devout Christian. I remember peeping into her bedroom once on my way to the bathroom and was impressed by the big crucifix on the wall, with a prayer stool beneath it. It made me feel she was a very special lady, very different from other people I knew, who had a deep relationship with God and she encouraged me to join the church choir where she was organist.

Little did I realize at the time just how valuable those weekly sessions were to be to me in later years – I feel she would be proud to know that I now pass on that kind of dis-cipline and learning to a younger generation, both as a peripatetic tutor at Lincoln Cathedral School and organising music clubs at my own children's junior schools and, of course, instilling in my three young sons a love of making music.

The other memorable characteristic of Miss Du Plat Taylor's could not be perpetu-ated today. She never took to driving a car, but was a familiar figure on her moped – kit-ted out in helmet and goggles for the journey from Horcott to the Market Place. When she arrived at the Coln House School crossroads she would dismount, hold her gauntleted hand up high to halt the oncoming traffic and proceed at a ladylike pace pushing her moped across the road and would only drop her arm to signal the traffic could continue once she was safely mounted again. What a star!

Katherine Mitchell

Still Crying

I took on the voluntary post of Town Crier for a fortnight – that was in 1975 and here I am, still crying more than a quarter century later. I won the Cirencester Heritage Year Town Criers' competition – well, I was the only one as entered. An old neighbour kitted me up with some sort of odds and ends that looked quaint enough to make me stand out; not as I need that now, 'cos folks describe me as a larger than life figure – although I've

Maurice Jones in good voice as a choirboy.

Maurice, still hitting the high notes leading a Town Criers Festival competition at the Millennium.

127

lost a bit and am down to 21 stone with a 52 inch chest but I am 6ft tall so that spreads it about a bit. Anyway, I did a bit of crying for school fêtes and things locally, then Rackhams in Cirencester asked me to shout in the streets about a sale they had going on. I was asked what my fee would be, so I said it would be the manager's hat – well, I knew he was a councillor and I thought his black tricorne was just about right for the job, then I 'charged' a haberdashery a bolt of red cloth for my services – and that made my first cloak.

I was officially appointed Fairford Town Crier in 1983 and am a member of the Ancient and Honourable Guild of Town Criers. I am thrilled to bits to have the bell that old Jack Jordan used when he was the Crier – his son brought it to me after his dad had passed on. My official dress now is based on the early eighteenth-century style, to be in keeping with the first recorded Town Crier here. Our mum said I got my love of dressing up from our dad – he used to have his own morris dancers team, but I don't reckon I could trip the light fantastic as well. I like music though – I used to have piano lessons with Margaret Norman up at Horcott Farm, I used to go with Johnnie Westbury, but he did better than I did – he got good enough to play proper tunes. Miss Norman was the choirmistress as well, so she got me to join the choir, then my voice broke, so Dave Pitts and I took up bell-ringing, we used to cycle all over the place to ring. Folks are tickled pink to have a Town Crier here, I know one American nearly got killed taking my photo. He was dead set to get a picture of me in front of the church when it was all foggy in the background – course, he led on the road to get the full church in and very near got run over. I 'ollared out just in time – that was one blessing of being able to shout loud!

I tell you, that red suit has changed my life: I'd never gone out of Fairford otherwise, but I've been all over the place crying in championships – even to South Africa, let alone on the continent, and last year we held the first championship here, more than thirty criers that day came from all over the country – the biggest number recorded for a British competition. Oyez!

Maurice Jones